Seumas O'Kelly

THE IRISH WRITERS SERIES

James F. Carens, General Editor

TITLE	AUTHOR
Sean O'Casey	Bernard Benstock
J. C. Mangan	James Kilroy
W. R. Rodgers	Darcy O'Brien
Standish O'Grady	Philip L. Marcus
Austin Clarke	John Jordan
Brian Friel	D. E. S. Maxwell
Daniel Corkery	George Brandon Saul
Eimar O'Duffy	Robert Hogan
Frank O'Connor	James Matthews
George Moore	Janet Egleson
James Joyce	Fritz Senn
John Butler Yeats	Douglas Archibald
Lord Edward Dunsany	Zack Bowen
Maria Edgeworth	James Newcomer
Mary Lavin	Zack Bowen
Oscar Wilde	Edward Partridge
Paul Vincent Carroll	Paul A. Doyle
Seumas O'Kelly	George Brandon Saul
Sheridan LeFanu	Michael Begnal
Somerville and Ross	John Cronin
Susan Mitchell	Richard M. Kain
J. M. Synge	Robin Skelton
Katharine Tynan	Marilyn Gaddis Rose
Liam O'Flaherty	James O'Brien
Iris Murdoch	Donna Gerstenberger

SEUMAS O'KELLY

George Brandon Saul

LEWISBURG
BUCKNELL UNIVERSITY PRESS

© 1971 by Associated University Presses, Inc.
Library of Congress Catalogue Card Number: 74-126030

Associated University Presses, Inc.
Cranbury, New Jersey 08512

ISBN: 0-8387-7765-1 (cloth)
0-8387-7661-2 (paper)
Printed in the United States of America

Also by George Brandon Saul

The Cup of Sand (Verse)
Bronze Woman (Verse)
A. E. Coppard: His Life and His Poetry . . .
The Wedding of Sir Gawain and Dame Ragnell (Trans.)
Major Types in English Literature (Outline Text)
Unimagined Rose (Verse)
"Only Necessity . . ." (Verse)
King Noggin (Children's Tale)
Selected Lyrics
The Elusive Stallion (Essays)
October Sheaf (Verse)
The Shadow of the Three Queens (Trad. Irish Lit. & Its
    Backgrounds)
Handbook of English Grammar and Writing Conventions
Stephens, Yeats, and Other Irish Concerns
Prolegomena to the Study of Yeats's Poems
Prolegomena to the Study of Yeats's Plays
The Age of Yeats (Anthology)
Four Songs (Words & Music)
Owls' Watch (Anthol. of Short Stories)
In . . . Luminous Wind (Essays on Yeats)
Quintet: Essays on Five American Women Poets
The Wild Queen (Novella)

Rushlight Heritage: Reflections on Selected Irish Short-Story Writers of the Yeatsian Era

Hound and Unicorn: Collected Verse—Lyrical, Narrative, and Dramatic

Carved in Findruine (Short Stories on Old Irish Themes)

Concise Introduction to Types of Literature in English

A Little Book of Strange Tales

Withdrawn in Gold (Essays on Stephens, Hodgson, & Dinesen)

c.1

To Alphonsus and Peggy Sweeney, and to Nora Duff

Contents

Acknowledgments

Without the support of a research grant from the University of Connecticut and the courtesies of various Irish friends, this monograph would scarcely have been possible; and I am duly grateful—as I am to my wife for assistance in checking and collating the most vexed conglomeration of MSS and TSS, often only partially extant and almost hopelessly intermingled, I have ever seen.

More specifically, I wish especially to thank Mr. Alphonsus Sweeney, of Dun Laoghaire, to whom I was referred by Padraic Colum, for innumerable kindnesses, and especially for making available the mass of O'Kelly reliques which were his inheritance; and Sister Anne Francis (Cavanaugh), of Mercyhurst College, Erie, Pennsylvania, for seven or eight bibliographical citations of periodical publication. (I found Sister engaged on a doctoral study of O'Kelly at University College when I arrived in Dublin; her dissertation, in progress—I understand—at date of writing, will doubtless present a point of view with its own claim to interest.)

Others deserving, for one reason or another, my gratitude include the staff of the National Library of Ireland, invariably helpful and cooperative in every way, as well as that of Trinity College, Dublin, and that of the Reference Department of the University of Connecticut; Mr. F. B. Singleton, Librarian of the Manchester *Guardian;* the custodians of vital statistics at the Dublin Custom House; Father Michael H. O'Callaghan, Administrator, The Presbytery, Loughrea, Co. Galway; Father Dermot Byrne, President, St. Joseph's College, Garbally Park, Ballinasloe; Professor Seán Ó Dochartaigh, of Galway; Mr. Micheál ó hAodha, Productions Director, Radio Telefís Éireann; Mr. W. B. Britton, editor of the *Leinster Leader;* Dr. Roger McHugh and Mr. Eamonn Grennan, University College, Dublin; Mr. A. J. Fitzpatrick, of *Independent Newspapers Ltd.* (Dublin) ; the late Mr. John Chichester, of the Museum Bookshop, Dublin; Mr. James A. Healy, of New York; and Mr. Desmond Rushe, of *Irish Newspapers, Ltd.,* Dublin.

Finally, for making my wife and me especially happy during our stay in Ireland, let me particularly thank Mr. Sweeney's charming wife, Peggy, and equally delightful children; and—last but not least—the staff of Buswell's Hotel, Dublin, whose Chairman of the Board, Mrs. Nora Duff, will always have a peculiarly warm spot in our hearts.

Seumas O'Kelly:
Chronology of Key Dates

?1875–?1878–? Born to Michael and Catherine Kelly, Mobhill, Loughrea, on now-indeterminable date; after father's retirement, family removed to Latimer Lodge (Loughrea).

Scanty education, during unestablished periods, at John Fury's "hedge-school" and St. Brendan's College, Loughrea.

1903: Editor, Skibbereen *Southern Star.*

1906: *By the Stream of Killmeen.* Editor, *Leinster Leader.*

1907: *The Matchmakers* produced 13 December by Theatre of Ireland.

1908: *The Matchmakers* published. *The Flame on the Hearth* (lost play) produced 24 November at the Abbey by the Theatre of Ireland.

1909: *The Shuiler's Child* produced 29 April at Dublin Rotunda by Theatre of Ireland and published.

1910: *The Home-Coming* produced 28 March by Theatre of Ireland. *The Shuiler's Child* produced 24 November by Abbey company.

1911: Likely period of rheumatic fever.

1912: *Three Plays.* Initial contributions to *Manchester Guardian.* Editor, *Dublin Saturday Post.*

1913: *Lustre* written in collaboration with Count Casimir de Markievicz, according to O'Kelly. *The Bribe* produced at Abbey, 18 December.

1914: *The Bribe.*

1915: Ill health forces resignation from *Dublin Saturday Post* and from briefer succeeding editorship of *Sunday Freeman. Driftwood* produced in London.

1916: Retirement to brother Michael's home, Naas. Editor, *Leinster Leader,* during Michael's incarceration as an officer of the Irish Volunteers. Invited to contribute "topical articles" to *Sunday Independent.*

1917: *The Lady of Deerpark* and *Waysiders. The Parnellite* produced at Abbey, 24 September.

1918: *Ranns & Ballads. ?The Leprechaun of Killmeen* (date uncertain). Editor of *Nationality* after Griffith's arrest. Died 14 November, after an invasion of the Sinn Féin premises. Huge funeral, 17 November.

1919: *Meadowsweet* (published this year) produced 7 October at the Abbey. *The Parnellite. The Golden Barque and The Weaver's Grave.*

1921: *Hillsiders.*

1922: *Wet Clay.*

Seumas O'Kelly

The Life

In a characteristically charming and warm-hearted tribute in *Essays and Recollections,* Seumas O'Sullivan, the poet who gave Dublin the most fascinating literary magazine of its day, recalls Seumas O'Kelly as "a stoutly-built little man . . . who seemed to me, at first sight, to be the most good-natured-looking person I had ever seen (and I may add that on this occasion my first impression was correct). . . . And never . . . did I hear a harsh word spoken by him, or of him. . . . His was . . . one of those very rare natures which have the faculty of spreading a sense of well-being, of security, good-fellowship, healing, by their very presence. Bitterness seemed to fade out in the presence of Seumas O'Kelly, and quarrelling was impossible when he was in the company. I can still hear that pleasant voice, see the almost priestly gesture of his hand as he said, 'That will be all right.' Yet beneath that gentleness lay hidden a very real strength. . . ." This tribute chimes with everything I have heard or read about O'Kelly—as for example with Maud Griffith's tenderness when she says, in a letter to his sister Nora (12 November 1919), "I am not forgetting your loved

15

dead this week and am having mass said, though I am sure he is happy, he was always so gentle and kind." Nevertheless, recorded factual detail about the career of this writer who has been called "Ireland's most neglected genius," seems sparse enough—and in character rather general, though never uncorroborative of his amazing industry or his "noble character and self-sacrificing life."

A son of Michael and Catherine Kelly, he was born in his parents' Mobhill, Loughrea, premises. Precisely when he was born can not be asserted with comfortable assurance in the absence of *undisputed* birth, and of *any* baptismal and educational, records. Assertedly the youngest of seven, if not eight, children, he is believed by the nephew he helped to rear to have been seven years younger than his brother Michael, who, according to birth certificate, was born 6 March 1873. There *is* a certified record of the birth of a son James (="Seumas") to Seumas' parents on 16 November 1875, but the nephew in question is certain this child died in early infancy, though no record of death exists. (Even if it did the problem of name would remain because the likelihood of Irish parents' naming a child after his dead brother or sister is very remote.) If Seumas O'Kelly's death certificate is correct in giving his age as forty, he must of course have been born in 1878 and could have been only five years younger than Michael despite his nephew's recollection; if Dublin Custom House records, aside from the death certificate, are complete and fully accurate, the birth year must have been 1875.

What need not be questioned is the fact that O'Kelly

came paternally of many generations engaged in "the milling and corn-carrying trade," "Kelly's Mills" standing in the townland of Leitrim, near Loughrea, a town of early thirteenth-century, Anglo-Norman founding, to the south of which is discernible, standing between Clare and Galway, Slieve Aughty—Yeats's "Echtge of streams." It is recorded that "family changes and intermarriage led to alteration in the ownership of the [Kelly] mills, and to the migration of some of the family to Loughrea where they continued the corn-buying and carrying trade" prosperously: the *Connacht Tribune* for 17 August 1935 speaks of their nigh-on-a-century-conducted "dual business of malting and bacon curing."

O'Kelly's parents were reputed "highly cultured and remarkable." His mother was originally Catherine Fitzgerald, of Foxhall, Loughrea: member of a notably hospitable family long since died out, and a woman remembered by her grandson as one so pious that, to win the grace of a happy death, she abstained from eating meat on Wednesdays as well as Fridays; and it is recorded in the *Leinster Leader* for 16 November 1918 that his father was "one of sufferers amongst the evicted tenants of the Clonrickarde estate." In any event, after a successful career in what was during the mid-nineteenth century a notable brewing and weaving center, he sold his business and retired to Latimer Lodge (Loughrea) with his wife, his children "Nora" (Honoria), Michael, and "Seumas" (James), and his grandson "Alphie" (Alphonsus Sweeney) ; he was to survive into 1912.

The Loughrea (named for the "gray lake" lying beside it) of the elder Kelly's business years, the years of Seumas' boyhood, must, with its town crier punctuating its rustic quietude, have had at least a degree of rural charm. At any rate, as O'Hanlon remarked in the *Irish Independent* for 1 March 1947, it permitted Seumas O'Kelly "intimate contact with the people of the West, with farmers, tinkers, fisher-folk, gombeen-men and the decaying ascendancy. He saw at first hand one of the bitterest upheavals in Irish history—the Land War; and he came to realise in that barren countryside why the land-hunger was such a fierce, integral part of the Irish peasant." Not least significantly, it stimulated his imagination with its ancient *Cloon na Morav,* "the Meadow of the Dead" at its eastern border; its not-distant Killmeen; and its lake, which—as both fact and symbol—was to haunt him through life.

Delicate as a child (and destined never to become "really robust") , O'Kelly conceivably found the rustic isolation of Loughrea conducive to his childhood invention of tales recounting visits to fairyland mounted on a gray steed, so that often a request for a story was put to him in the form of an inquiry as to whether he had been out on this steed the night before. Other boyhood inventions concerned " 'The White Lady' who used to haunt the lake side at night"; while a favorite character was a fairy he called "Lanty-cant"—a name which, according to his brother Michael, on whose preface to *The Parnellite* I am drawing, later appeared mysteriously as the caption "to a story in a Dublin publication." Meanwhile youthful experience included service as an acolyte at the Abbey Church of the local Carmelite

Monastery, reflections of which are supposed to be discernible in "The Sick Call" (*Waysiders*) and a piece of verse, "In Memoriam," commemorating Lay Brother Joseph O'Shea.

Available general, as distinguished from religious, education seems to have been meager enough. From what the *Connacht Tribune* (17 August 1935) called a "humble hedge-school, conducted by John Fury at the eastern point of Cabbage-lane," O'Kelly proceeded to St. Brendan's College (Loughrea), which later became by transfer St. Joseph's, Garbally Park, Ballinasloe. Here he is said to have proved, as an undistinguished student, "a thorn and difficulty" to both the president, Fr. M. J. Leahy, and the faculty members. What his subjects of study were can be merely a matter of speculation: on 8 May 1967 Fr. Dermot Byrne, head of St. Joseph's, said in a personal letter that St. Brendan's "was conducted in a private house in Loughrea and whatever registers were kept at the time cannot now be found," adding "I am afraid that the school was a very informal institution . . . simply a pioneer effort at providing some education on the part of one or two priests." In this connection one may remark that O'Kelly's story "Padna Mitches," concerning a boy's playing hooky one day from "St. Austin's Seminary," strongly suggests the autobiographical: indeed, one untitled Sweeney manuscript which is clearly the original draft of this story calls the school "St. Brendan's." But whatever the limitations of his formal education, O'Kelly had picked up Irish by listening to his elders; and time was to turn him into an avid reader (with an eventual special fondness for Whitman and

Jack London, according to his nephew). Another developing interest was that in birds and flowers, as various fugitive essays of his maturity attest.

Ruminating on the scant references to O'Kelly's early years just summarized, one remembers an untitled one-page Sweeney manuscript of verse reminiscent of a boy-hood friendship and testifying to the central importance of the "gray lake" to his experience and imagination. During the boating referred to, he recalls

> I saw the little island well,
> Circled by rock and reed and shell,
> Where we were wont to moor our craft
> And tell each other, hopeful, daft,
> Of all the strange things that we'd do
> When half the wide world we'd review.
> And I remember with what scorn
> We raked the town where we were born—

But there is no specific identification of the friend—any more than there is of the girl addressed in a love lyric entitled "To Elis" among the Sweeney manuscripts, though Mr. Sweeney suspects that "Elis" may be a disguise for "Katie Dougherty," whom he counted of special interest to his uncle before her early death. (One speculates also on "An Ologone.") Incidentally, the only rumored amorous, though possibly shy, inclination of O'Kelly was toward the beautiful actress Máire Nic Shiubhlaigh (*Mary,* sister of Frank, *Walker*).

More compelling than love appears to have been the early drive toward journalism, which was eventually to lead to lifelong friendships with such men as J. W. O'Beirne, Dublin journalist and nationalist; Arthur

Griffith, founder of Sinn Féin and editor of its succes-
sive organs; and—above all—Seumas O'Sullivan (*James
Starkey*) , to whom O'Kelly was introduced by Griffith.

The journalistic activity is said by Malone, writing in
the *Dublin Magazine* for July-September 1930, to have
begun very early when a newspaper was founded "in
an adjoining county." Initial contributions appear to
have been the youthful "Jottings" in the *Tuam News,*
which led to editorship of the *Midland Tribune* before
(it has been claimed) O'Kelly turned eighteen; and it
is worth recalling with Malone that as a journalist
O'Kelly tried "to reform, and to shake out of the petti-
ness in which they seemed to be deeply sunk" the provincial newspapers with which he became associated.
Significantly, too, his work permitted him to exploit his
"deep and active interest in the several movements for
the regeneration of his country. He was an ardent sup-
porter of the Gaelic League and industrial revival movements," and—according to the *Leinster Leader* of 16
November 1918—one of the first to support Arthur
Griffith when he "founded the Sinn Féin organization."
And his performance shortly induced an offer of the
editorship of the Cork *Weekly Sun,* though circum-
stances led to the lapsing thereof before acceptance. In
1903 he went to the *Southern Star,* of Skibbereen, Co.
Cork—reputedly the youngest editor in Ireland. Curiously enough, however, recorded factual detail does not
thenceforth become so voluminous as one might have ex-
pected.

N.L. MS 2112 has a letter of 1 December 1904 which
seems to imply that O'Kelly was then lodging in Skib-

bereen; and it was apparently during this year, or a little earlier, that he began contributing to *The United Irishman* and *The Irish Packet*—in that order. On 22 October 1905, according to information received from his nephew, his mother was taken ill while saying the Stations of the Cross in Loughrea Cathedral. Removed to Latimer Lodge in a coma, she died there the next day. It was a shocking blow to O'Kelly, who was in Skibbereen at the time; whether the manuscript lyric "In Memory (Autumn 1906)" relates to his mother is another matter for speculation. His nephew, incidentally, preserves a letter from him to Nora dated 17 January 1905, though it is biographically of no consequence. During the year in reference, O'Kelly seems to have made his earliest appearances in *The Irish Rosary* and the *Irish Weekly Independent,* and probably to have finished assembling his first book, *By the Stream of Killmeen,* published in August of the following year.

Approval of this weak first collection by the Irish press almost passes credibility: not only the *Southern Star,* which labeled the author "brilliant," but more than a dozen other newspapers, including *Sinn Féin* (which recognized at one point a touch "worthy of Turgenieff"), gave fulsome approval, their reviewers generally impressed by O'Kelly's capacity for sympathetic character-presentation. Of these journals, the *New Ireland Review* (October 1906) did criticize his "constant aiming after literary effect," but credited him with "knowledge, such as few writers have, of the Irish people."

The year 1906 also saw O'Kelly initiating his longest

single journalistic connection when he became editor of the *Leinster Leader,* published at Naas, Co. Kildare, as well as beginning his contributions to *Sinn Féin,* which made its initial appearance 5 May. The *Leader,* its motto "Fides et Patria," was normally an eight-page paper datelined for Saturday issue, but actually on sale Fridays, so that O'Kelly would "put it to bed" Thursday nights. Since the paper employed only one mature and one junior reporter, O'Kelly had little time for idling, but did, on the other hand, find opportunity to buy and publish some of the early work of emerging Irish writers.

It is said that on assuming this editorship, O'Kelly first took private rooms in Main Street with an O'Neill family. Presently he acquired "Abbeyville," a four-chimney house standing not many feet west of the canal lock and permitting observation later put to use in his "Golden Barque" stories. After furnishing this house with new pieces, he brought his father, his sister Nora, and his nephew to live with him in 1907. Meanwhile he had joined the Naas Sinn Féin Club; and presently he began being intermittently host to many Republicans, including the Countess Markievicz, who attended the yearly June commemorations at Wolfe Tone's grave in Bodenstown, about five miles from Naas. On weekends he would make the short trip to Dublin to meet his friends at Webb's Bookshop, Crampton Quay on the Liffey. There Griffith (whose interest *By the Stream of Killmeen* is said to have induced) introduced him to O'Sullivan, who is responsible for noting, in the volume earlier referred to, that his rheumatic fever, entailing residual heart damage but leaving him "an indefatigable worker" nevertheless, was "contracted in Naas," though precisely when (?1911) is in question.

Another unanswered question is posed by a 5 December 1906 letter (N.L. MS 2112) addressed to O'Kelly at Naas by Cassell and Co., London, offering only doubtful encouragement to submit a short-story manuscript even though its component tales were linked with each other. The question is, What manuscript? The only conceivable one satisfying the descriptive terms of the letter would seem to be that of *The Leprechaun of Killmeen,* though O'Kelly did not begin serial publication of this work until 5 December 1908.

The year 1907, which may just possibly have seen O'Kelly's collaboration with Count Casimir de Markievicz on the one-act play *Lustre,* though the date is seriously in question and O'Kelly was eventually to recall it as 1913, seems mainly memorable in his career for the production of his one-act comedy *The Matchmakers* on 13 December by The Theatre of Ireland, in whose organization he had had a hand. Happily this production by a group of dedicated amateurs who received no remuneration for their work was auspicious. Máire Nic Shiubhlaigh recalls that some of the audience, "annoyed . . . because the story dealt with a 'made marriage,' came prepared to register their disapproval on the first night," but ended with "congratulations and apologies"; and the *Freeman's Journal* (14 December 1907) records the initial performance as "a distinct success, the house [the Abbey Theatre] being kept in continuous outbursts of laughter" and O'Kelly being given a curtain

call. Dublin's professional playgoing diarist, J. Holloway, whose manuscripts are in the National Library of
Ireland, found the first production (preceded by that
of Æ's *Deirdre*) somewhat unsatisfactory, the play itself
amusing but verbose. But even he counted the 30 December production a tremendous success. The play's
persistent appeal is evident from the fact that O'Kelly
told Ernest Boyd in a letter of 30 June 1915 (Healy)
that *The Matchmakers* had "been played by amateur
societies in every county in Ireland."

O'Kelly's next play to reach the stage was another one-
acter, *The Flame on the Hearth,* on 24 November 1908
(in which year *The Matchmakers* was first published),
at the Abbey, again through The Theatre of Ireland.
This production was apparently not satisfactory, despite
the approval of Holloway (apparently fascinated by the
beauty and acting of Mary Walker in the role of the
young mother), though the one at the Rotunda on 19
March 1909 came off better. O'Kelly—according to a 30
June 1915 letter to Ernest Boyd—eventually reworked
this play, of which no manuscript or typescript has been
located, into the seemingly never-produced *The
Stranger.* One can only wonder whether *The Flame* . . .
is the same with "The Sleep of the Stranger," about
which Fred Morrow wrote on 3 November 1908 to
query O'Kelly's wishes for production (N.L. MS 2112).

The Shuiler's Child, said to have been written for
Mary Walker (like Maud Gonne, something of a beautiful revolutionary: she was to be with the Cumann na
mBan at Jacob's Factory during the Easter Rising),
reached the stage 29 April 1909, at the Rotunda (Dub-

lin) , though it was presumably put into approximately
final form in 1907, if we may accept the implications of
a 9 January 1908 letter from Padraic Colum asking to
see it. Amusingly disapproved of, as a third near-success,
for both acting and lack of certain dramatic desiderata
(though granted verisimilitude and characters) by the
gabbling Holloway, it was actually a remarkable success
(and the first of O'Kelly's plays to qualify for subsequent
production by the Abbey company, when the *Evening
Telegraph* for 25 November 1910 recorded a triple recall of the cast, with applause that "swelled into cheer-
ing," at its conclusion) : a success reechoed when Mary
Walker emerged from retirement to revive it on 14
April 1948 for the Masque Theatre at Ozanam Hall,
Dublin. Directed by Fred Morrow, it was approved by
the *Irish Independent* (30 April 1909) as "powerful" in
its presentation of a shuiler, and strongly endorsed by
such journals as the *Evening Mail* (30 April 1909) and
the *Evening Telegraph* (1 May 1909) . And one gathers
that Mary Walker as the shuiler and Constance Markievicz as Cecelia Stoney proved outstanding in a generally
excellent cast. In later years, Ernest Boyd, in *The Contemporary Drama of Ireland,* was to recall that "as por-
trayed by Miss Maire nic Shiubhlaigh [Mary Walker],
the tragic figure of Moll Woods was one of the most
memorable in the history of the Irish Theatre." Miss
Walker herself, recalling (*The Splendid Years,* p. 79)
that James Stephens played the part of Tim O'Halloran
in the original production (though he had his name
given as "Stephen James" on the program!) , names this
"undoubtedly the most successful play presented by"

The Theatre of Ireland and says that O 'Kelly admitted
to her that it was as a result of his having seen the segment concerning the gipsy woman in Act 4 of Ibsen's
Brand (Miss Walker having played the part of this
woman in the 6 December 1906 Theatre of Ireland production of the play) that he wrote *The Shuiler's Child,*
hailed by *Sinn Féin* (8 May 1909) as the "finest char-
acter-study seen on the stage in Dublin for several years,
and the only play written by a living Irishman about the
life of our day which can be called tragedy." One might
add that after the Abbey production, Holloway was
willing to concede its power, though even Mary Walker's
sweetness and sincerity as Mrs. Ford did not alter his
opinion that O'Kelly's next play to reach the boards,
The Home-Coming (which even the author designated
merely "A Curtain-Raiser"—though he published it in
both *Three Plays* and *Waysiders*), was anything more
than a triviality indebted to *The Gaol Gate* and *The
Building Fund.*

O'Kelly's industry during the period of play-produc-
tion just indicated, roughly 1907–10, was almost incredible. For aside from editing the *Leinster Leader,* he was
writing and publishing verse and short stories—the latter
in quantity. Most of this creative work went into the
Irish Weekly Independent, in which the stories collected
in *Hillsiders* and *The Leprechaun of Killmeen* first appeared, as well as "At the Burning of the Sod," a series
of tales sequential to the latter but never presented in
book form. Another favored outlet for publication was
Sinn Féin, in which not only miscellaneous verse but
the great "Can with the Diamond Notch," eventually to

open *Waysiders,* first appeared. Whether or not the long romance *Edain,* of which the opening six chapters alone were printed in the *Weekly Freeman* several years after O'Kelly's death, was also written during the period in reference (if not, indeed, as technical considerations tempt one to suspect, earlier) is a matter for speculation.

Because of an almost total lapse in the appearance of new creative work during 1911, Vivian Mercier suggests in his doctoral thesis that O'Kelly suffered his attack of rheumatic fever, leading to recurrent ill health, "probably in this year," and the speculation seems not unreasonable. Certainly there was an upsurge of activity the following year, when O'Kelly issued his verse broadside and his *Three Plays,* and began his contributions to the Manchester *Guardian* (which according to his nephew offered him a place on its staff which he decided not to accept after an interview in Manchester). Significantly, too, he left the *Leinster Leader,* having been appointed editor of the *Dublin Saturday Post.* His brother Michael succeeded him on the *Leader,* moving temporarily into "Abbeyville" before taking up residence at "Gleann-na-Greine," where he maintained his father, who died the following year in Richmond Hospital, Dublin, with burial on 26 October. Meanwhile O'Kelly had moved to "Avondale," 6 Home Farm Road, Drumcondra, taking his sister Nora with him (his nephew being then away at school, though presently rejoining his aunt and uncle and resuming his education in Dublin).

According to Alphonsus Sweeney, he and O'Kelly attended the November 1913 meeting for the organization

of the Irish Volunteers held at the Rotunda, Dublin;
but of course, the great event of the year was the Lennox
Robinson production of *The Bribe* at the Abbey on 18
December, though Holloway records the author's obvious sadness at not—two days before the première—
having been invited to any of the rehearsals.

The Bribe was another pronounced success, with Nora
Desmond playing Mrs. Diamond; Kathleen Drago,
Mary Kirwan; Eileen O'Doherty, Mrs. Kirwan; Arthur
Sinclair, John Kirwan; and Fred O'Donovan, Dr. Luke
Diamond—to mention just a handful of the very com-
petent cast. *The Stage* (24 December 1913) called it a
"serious advance" in O'Kelly's art, in an opinion shared
by *Irish Life* (26 December 1913). Papers ranging from
the *Tuam News* to the *Irish Times* applauded; "The
Stage" Year Book for 1914 called it "the play of the
year"—an opinion reiterated by W. J. Lawrence after
a praiseful lecture by Professor Magennis to the National Literary Society, Dublin, at which the chairman,
Dr. L. C. Purser, went so far as to crown it (cf. the *Evening Telegraph* for 9 March 1915) "the play of the
Abbey." But revival of the play on 22 November 1943,
one must unhappily add, brought only generally, rather
than uniformly, favorable critical reactions, as for example those of "The Critic" in the *Sunday Independent*
for 28 November.

Book-publication of *The Bribe* in 1914 was another
happy occasion for O'Kelly. *The British Review* (June
1914) called it frankly "more nervous and beautiful"
than any contemporary English drama, praising its presentation of Irish character in "its intense realism, its

raking humour, its primitiveness," though in "tenderly sympathetic" fashion; the "Literary Supplement" of the *Irish Times* (28 May 1914) approved it as "at least a minor tragedy . . . a rare achievement"; and the *Irish News and Belfast Morning News* (11 April 1914) endorsed it in a long review by "Dunbwee." Only the *Athenæum* (11 April 1914) among major voices gave qualified praise, counting it less "effective" than *The Shuiler's Child,* with "the last act . . . more in the nature of an appendix than of a climax."

The year 1915 was again critical for O'Kelly. Ill health forced him to relinquish the editorship of the *Dublin Saturday Post:* on 29 October, five former colleagues wrote sending him a gift in token of friendship and expressing their regret over his leaving, with best wishes for the recovery of his health to permit fulfillment of promised literary success. But he made one more brief attempt (lasting two weeks, he wrote Boyd on 6 January 1916: Healy) at regular employment—as editor of the *Sunday Freeman*—before capitulating to medical advice and giving up the Drumcondra home in January of 1916 to return to Naas with his sister and nephew to live with his brother Michael, transporting disguised as trees—according to his nephew—some of the rifles earlier landed at Howth by Erskine Childers and temporarily hidden in the piano at 6 Home Farm Road. Meanwhile it would appear that he must have made a trip to England, where—in Manchester and London, successively—his play *Driftwood* was performed: at least, there is preserved, in N.L. MS 2112, a letter of 12 October 1915 addressed to him at 52 Acacia Road, St.

John's Wood, London N.W., by Douglas Gordon, producer of the play at Manchester's Gaiety Theatre, speaking of its great success. By 29 December, Gordon was addressing him at Drumcondra.

Though one of his weaker plays, *Driftwood* (written by 30 June 1915: Healy) was clearly not unsuccessful in either Manchester or London. True, *The Stage* did suggest the dialogue required revising and the Manchester *Guardian* had reservations ("The talkiness of it all was baffling, and . . . whatever 'Driftwood' may be, it is not a play") ; but general approval came from the *Star,* the *Standard,* the *Observer,* the *Manchester Courier,* the *Daily Despatch,* the *Morning Post,* the *Evening Telegraph,* the *Pall Mall Gazette,* the *Evening News,* and the *Evening Chronicle.* And a letter to Ernest Boyd (26 August 1915: Healy) suggests O'Kelly thought he had done a good job on the characters of dramatist and critic.

In January 1916 O'Kelly's nephew joined the Naas Company of Irish Volunteers, of which Michael O'Kelly was commanding officer. Both were arrested on 29 April, after the Easter Rising, and deported to Wakefield Gaol. Seumas O'Kelly resumed the editorship of the *Leader* until Michael's release in August, his work complicated by his having to get all controversial articles passed by the censor in Dublin Castle to prevent not only personal trouble but the possible destruction of printing equipment by sledgehammer. His nephew, released by the British because he was under eighteen, recalls that at the time of arrest the following exchange took place:

Seumas O'Kelly: "I suppose you'll take the canary, too?"
British Agent: "Why?"
S. O'K.: "Because he's an alien—a German canary!"

After his brother's return to Naas and resumption of
his editorship, O'Kelly appears to have relapsed into
calmer, though creatively no less industrious, living. On
25 November an editorial invitation to submit "topical
articles" arrived from the *Sunday Independent,* to
which he contributed heavily in the months ahead, not
infrequently making duplicate appearances in the Manchester *Guardian* and producing a number of manuscripts in prose and verse which had to await posthumous publication in the periodicals. In September
of 1917 he both published *The Lady of Deerpark* and
saw his play *The Parnellite* produced by the Abbey
Company to the tune of a genuine ovation. And October brought *Waysiders,* one of his really important
collections of stories (though one earlier-published
play was included), in which was assembled material
dating back to early 1910 in periodical issue.

The Parnellite, which had its roots in the "No-rent
Manifesto of 1881"—the "Land League" days, won even
Holloway's approval. The *Irish Times* (25 September)
called it "a distinct advance on his previous work,"
while recognizing "a tendency towards melodrama."
Irish Life (28 September) echoed approval, at the same
time observing that "it never was the usual thing to
find an unswerving Parnellite hounded to death by his
anti-Parnellite fellow-countrymen"; while the *Freeman's Journal* (25 September) countered such endorse-
ment as that of the *Dublin Saturday Post* (29 Septem-

ber) by naming it "the creation of a novelist rather than a dramatist" and a work in need of "a good deal of pruning."

The novel and short stories seem to have received far less general attention than they clearly deserved—perhaps because World War I was still in progress when they were issued. Mercier, writing in the *Irish Times* for 9 September 1944, claims the former "passed almost unnoticed;" and Forrest Reid, in *Retrospective Adventures,* says O'Kelly admitted "it attracted little attention in Ireland and none at all elsewhere."

Some sound approval there fortunately was, though with minor qualifications. For example, the Manchester *Guardian* (in a review by "M.C." entitled "An Irish Turgenev?" and published 9 November 1917) describes it as "an Irish story with as near an approach to the manner of the Russian master as he could manage. . . . People move and think in a peculiarly limpid atmosphere, though they think in half-tones and move almost imperceptibly." It considers the characters other than Mary "strangely unreal," though "the sense of tragedy is surely kept." The *Irish Monthly* (November 1917) also counts the minor characters the less successful and feels that the writing is "uneven" and that the logical end of the story is Mary's death; nevertheless its review is basically favorable. And the *Irish Independent* (24 September 1917) also offers general praise, while asserting "there is manifest striving after melodramatic effect in the closing chapter that is altogether out of keeping with the level tone maintained throughout the rest of the work." Happily, there seems to have been no significant quibbling over the quality of *Waysiders:* certainly not in the reviews seen by the present writer. The Manchester *Guardian,* for instance, asserted flatly in its 8 December 1917 review that these stories "must be ranked high"; and such journals as the *Irish Times* and the *Irish Rosary* had been even earlier in emphatic approval. Meanwhile O'Kelly had already sent out his second major collection of tales: a 16 May letter from him to the Talbot Press, written from Gleann-na-Greine, Michael's home in Naas, urges a publishing decision on *Hillsiders.* Sadly enough, he did not live to see this book a reality.

To 1918 may possibly belong another lesser volume of tales, *The Leprechaun of Killmeen,* despite customary dating; the matter is considered below in §A of the annotated bibliography. This collection of relatively early material seems, whatever its absolute quality, to have been popular in its serialized form in the *Irish Weekly Independent* and was to be reprinted a decade or so later in *The Hearthstone.*

To 1918, the year in which Forrest Reid wrote agreeing to an exchange of books and sending three of his, certainly belongs *Ranns & Ballads,* O'Kelly's one collection of verse, arranged by him for issue despite the report in the *Sunday Independent* (19 October 1919) by Louis H. Victory, once his associate on the *Leinster Leader,* that he "had a very poor opinion of the quality of his own verses; persuasion and argument were seldom successful in inducing him to give them publicity." (Victory was perhaps limited in his knowledge of versifiers!) From a publisher's note in the book we learn that the manuscript was sent in less than two weeks before the author's death, which of course occurred before proofs were available.

As in the cases of *By the Stream of Killmeen* and the subsequent *Wet Clay,* reviewers' approval of this little book seems incredible: "S. O'C.," in *New Ireland* (22 February 1919), calls it "perhaps the most typical and comprehensive product of his own self"; the *Sunday Independent* (19 October 1919) names its author "one of the most brilliant of our 20th Century poets"! One can only suspect confusion of O'Kelly's poetic talent with his personal character—a character whose conscientious fineness, operating through devotion to Ireland, was in a sense the real cause of his early death.

For O'Kelly, despite medical warnings about the danger to his heart, had once more removed from Naas to Dublin to assume journalistic responsibilities, this time to take over the editorship of *Nationality* with its issue for 25 May 1918, because Arthur Griffith (who had foreseen and provided against the contingency) had been seized at home by the British the previous midnight and spirited to a warship lying at Kingstown (now Dun Laoghaire), where he was held incommunicado for deportation with numerous other Irish also taken on trumped-up charges of participation in a pretended "German plot." Whether or not Griffith showed much consideration for his friend's welfare in drafting him as editorial substitute seems to trouble commentators no more than it apparently bothered the selfless O'Kelly, who certainly committed himself completely in fulfilling his trust. The editorials which resulted underscore brilliantly his logical political mind, his clear view of history, his concern to comment on British abuses, his natural devotion to Sinn Féin as the best hope for Irish independence, his hope that President Wilson's stand for national self-determination would comprehend Ireland, and his faculty for quietly sardonic expression in a highly literate style—as when he says (1 June), "England has always been virtuous in Ireland. She has never throttled us except for our soul's salvation."

Meanwhile he was sharing lodgings with Seumas O'Sullivan, his closest friend, at 5 Ardenza Terrace, Seapoint, where the novelist Kickham had "passed his closing years." Daily, except Sundays, he would commute (cf. his essay "An Autumn Morning / From a Seaside Suburb to Dublin" in the *Sunday Independent,* 22 September 1918) to and from Dublin and the editorial office in Sinn Féin headquarters at 6 Harcourt Street.

Armistice Day was, so to say, the beginning of O'Kelly's end. According to his brother Michael (cf. "Homage to Seumas O'Kelly"), "On the third night [after the armistice had occurred] a crowd of drunken soldiers and the wives of soldiers serving at the front known as 'Separation Allowance Women' broke into the Sinn Féin premises, attacked the occupants, and proceeded to wreck the place. Seumas O'Kelly feebly defended himself with his walking stick, but when at length the row ceased, he was found lying unconscious. He was quickly removed to Jervis Street hospital but he never rallied and passed away at 5 in the morning [*i.e.,* of 14 November]." The death certificate, by the way, lists the cause of death as "Cerebral Haemorrhage / Coma."

Robert Brennan, it should be remarked, gives in *Allegiance* a colorful variant account of the tragic occurrence (though he clearly misdates both collapse and time of death). Whether his memory of the office scene (involving no attack on O'Kelly personally—as also none is implied in the *Evening Telegraph* report of 14 November) or Michael O'Kelly's description is the accurate record, his account of O'Kelly's distress at seeing Grafton Street heavily bedecked with Union Jacks and of his shortly succeeding collapse seems convincing enough. Incidentally, O'Hanlon (his final clause obviously inaccurate) records in *The Capuchin Annual, 1949* that "after offering feeble resistance, O'Kelly had to stand impotently by; but the incident was too much for him, and after the soldiers had left he was found dead at his desk."

Word of O'Kelly's death reached Griffith quickly, and *Nationality* for 23 November, then edited by J. J. Burke, contains his tribute in a 16 November letter from Gloucester Gaol:

> I have just heard of Seumas O'Kelly's death. It is a tragic loss to Ireland at this moment, and for me it is the loss of one of my dearest friends. He has given his life for the cause, for two years ago he was warned by the doctors that to expose himself to any excitement would lead to fatal results, but I knew well Seumas could not let "Nationality" lack for an Editor after my arrest. I hoped he would survive the strain. I cannot write more today.

It may be here remarked that O'Kelly's last issue of

Nationality ranged from the Dublin armistice celebration of the "English 'fly-boys'" to the threatening proposals of the British "Committee of Currency and Foreign Exchanges After the War"; and that his own last editorial (appropriately entitled "The Swan Song," though this heading was intended to relate to the Irish Provincialist Party) concerns Dillon and "his futility in the British House of Commons" and the Provincialist Party's appeal to President Wilson, putting him "in a false position."

Accounts of O'Kelly's funeral—that of a national hero rather than that of a writer—accounts sometimes precisely duplicative in part, are variously available: for example, in "The Late Mr. Seumas O'Kelly," *Leinster Leader,* 23 November 1918, and articles of the same caption in the *Irish Independent* and the *Freeman's Journal* for 18 November 1918. Ironically enough, these death notices represent the only detailed coverage of any segment of his history. The *Daily Sketch* for 20 November has a camera shot of the immense procession, which, with Sinn Féin in charge of arrangements, began at noon of 17 November at the Church of St. Teresa, in Dublin's Clarendon Street (where O'Kelly's brother Patrick, the Reverend Fr. Alphonsus, with several other Carmelite priests in attendance, had celebrated a Requiem Mass) and moved through crowd-lined streets to Glasnevin and the O'Kelly grave (No. 340, 540, Prospect Cemetery, Section St. Paul's).

The whole two-hour procession, which in one account is said to have taken place "in a torrential downpour," was as impressive as guaranteed by a coffin cov-

ered with the Irish Republican colors; large priestly
representation; honor guard of Irish Volunteers, cycling
police leading the cortege; marshaling of Sinn Féin and
Nationality executives and journalistic friends, and of
hundreds of members of Cumann na mBan and other
women's organizations, Gaelic Leaguers, boy and girl
scouts, and others; several bands; participation by the
Lord Mayor of Dublin; wreaths; and final service in the
mortuary chapel preceding prayers by Fr. Alphonsus at
the graveside, with a recitation of the Rosary in Irish
to which the crowd responded. Then it was over and
Ireland proceeded pretty well to forget one more of its
notable writers and humanitarians, though it is said
that the National Graves Association did erect a plaque
over his grave in a November 1939 ceremony. And the
twenty-fifth anniversary of his death *was* memorialized.
The Abbey revived *The Bribe;* there were tributes on
13 November in the *Irish Independent,* the *Irish Press,*
and the *Irish Times* (in the latter instance by Seumas
O'Sullivan, presenting material re-used in *Essays and
Recollections*) ; and on 16 November Radio Éireann
broadcast "Homage to Seumas O'Kelly," with a short
biographical talk supplied by Michael O'Kelly, as well
as several poems "spoken by Patricia Clancy, Robert
Mooney, and Liam Redmond," "The Sick Call" read by
Redmond, and a production by Gabriel Fallon of *The
Home-Coming,* with Peg Monahan, Patricia Clancy,
Liam Redmond, and Robert Mooney as the cast. But no
effort to keep in print O'Kelly's best creative work
(aside from one *novella*) was observable, despite the
pathetic prophecy of an anonymous writer in *The Gael*

for 28 August 1922, who asserted "No book of Seumas O'Kelly's will die in Ireland," even while admitting "that scarcely any other author, either dead or living, has had the misfortune to have his books so wretchedly produced."

Almost a year after O'Kelly's death, his one-act *Meadowsweet* was put on at the Abbey, and 1919 also brought publication of this play, as well as of *The Parnellite* and *The Golden Barque and The Weaver's Grave,* the latter containing the one story of O'Kelly's which has approximated anything suggestive of universal popularity. *Meadowsweet* (cf., *e.g.*, the *Evening Telegraph* and the *Evening Herald* for 8 October) was well received, with special praise for Arthur Shields's acting in the part of "Johnny." And the reception accorded the collection of prose tales might have been conceived as just comfort to the author's ghost. On 11 December 1919 Ernest Boyd, then with the Talbot Press, wrote to Nora saying, " 'The Weaver's Grave' is getting splendid reviews."

The just-named tale, which the *Liverpool Post* once called "a short story in a thousand" and Stephen Gwynn, in his article "Modern Irish Literature," was to term "the best short story in Irish literature," seems to have had a typical O'Kelly genesis. It is recorded that Fr. Alphonsus Kelly recalled on one occasion that a brother [obviously Michael] once told Seumas "that he had overheard a dispute between two old men as to the location of the grave," and that "Seumas, ever perceptive, took the story to his brain and wove a plot about it." In any event, it proved the major attraction of a book the

Manchester *Guardian* judged "the most promising thing that has come out of Ireland for some time," and a book whose critical approbation ranged from the *Evening Telegraph* (24 January 1920) to the *Sphere* (2 February 1920, the *Irish Statesman* (in a review by Reid: 6 December 1919), and the London *Times Literary Supplement* (20 November 1919) —though the last did, with a British dullness blinding it to O'Kelly's humorously fanciful intention, object to the spelling "barque" (which defines a vessel with "a particular sort of rigging") for designation of a canal boat!

Such, then, was the story (except for an undated form letter notifying O'Kelly of election to membership in the National Literary Society), so far as currently available material has made verifiable recollection possible. A few more posthumous publications should be noted. *Hillsiders,* another major volume, appeared in 1921, though its contents had apparently been assembled in 1917 from matter already eight years available. "Edain," which might have become a significant book, was partly issued in the *Weekly Freeman* in 1922, the year which also brought the novel *Wet Clay.* And in 1923 the play "Driftwood," whose 1915 production has had comment above, appeared in the *Dublin Magazine.*

Of these works, *Wet Clay* (a long-worked-over affair which one suspects would have received further cobbling if death had not intervened) appears to have stirred the most enthusiastic response—response so enthusiastic in spots as to pass seeming credibility. *Sunday Independent* and *New York Times* approval was compounded by *Young Ireland's* opinion (6 November

1922) that the book was "perfect" as a work of art. The *Irish Review* (23 December 1922) found in it "the purest realism" without morbidity—"as stark a tragedy as ever Hardy conceived, but . . . less depressing." *The Freeman's Journal* (16 December 1922), also extravagantly favorable in general, does admit that the characters "do not always bear strictest analysis" and asserts a Hardyesque pessimism, the love story having "sordid sides," so that "whether it is really a true revelation of Irish life may be doubted"! Despite which Stephen Gwynn, in an article already noted, calls it "one of the best among Irish novels," and Andrew Malone (*Dublin Magazine,* July–September 1930) counts it a sociologically faithful and "perfectly balanced" novel.

One wonders whether the dead author himself might not have smiled a bit skeptically at such extravagance.

The Works

A clear and balanced estimate of the work of any voluminous author, reasonable quality assumed, is never easy to achieve. In the case of a man like O'Kelly it is particularly difficult. Why, is the question. Perhaps the demands imposed on O'Kelly's time and energy as a Sinn Féiner and journalist were too heavy always to permit that leisurely reworking which seldom harms any author's inventions; perhaps more careful editorial handling, especially of the posthumous publications, was desirable, as I feel sure it was; perhaps the simple unevenness of O'Kelly's miscellaneous achievement has tended to blunt the lineaments of true genius shining behind its finest items. And of course, it is doubtless a kind of misfortune that O'Kelly's significance has been overshadowed by that of Yeats, Synge, and Stephens, justly and understandably enough, as well as by that of Joyce.

There are, of course, other reasons why O'Kelly's artistic image has been blemished, especially in the eyes of those not drawn to examine the whole because of occasional flaws in the parts: readers over-hasty to dismiss the genuine accomplishment because of what has been termed his "latent tendency to melodrama," his occasionally "platitudinous sentimentality"—both being charges which can to some degree be substantiated, perhaps because, as Malone—in the article last cited above—said, "Essentially the mind of Seumas O'Kelly was tragic, and it was the more sombre aspects of life that seemed to attract him." The melodramatic is often a temptation to such minds, and the melodramatic is apt to draw the sentimental in its wake. But the evidence of such fortunately rare bits of drivel as "Was It As Well?" (*i.e.,* that a young man should have drowned rather than forsaken Ireland for America!) may also suggest excess religiosity as the source of sentimental deviations. And indeed, there is also to be recognized the fact that other considerations as well, good and noble in themselves, may occasionally in O'Kelly's case, as in that of many another craftsman, have subverted art in favor of propaganda and didacticism. The patriot is rarely the poet, though the poet is often enough a patriot. What O'Kelly produced purely as a patriot and moralist is one thing; what he produced as a poet, in whatever literary medium, is another. The contrast lies between *The Parnellite* and *The Shuiler's Child,* between "The Revenge of Seaghan Buidhe" and "The Weaver's Grave," between "At the Burning of the Sod" and "The Gray Lake" or "The Can with the Diamond Notch."

The comment that follows is built on an implied effort to isolate that work of O'Kelly's which really counts as literature—all part of a mass of which Malone fairly remarks that it "owes a great deal to the memories of his Galway childhood, and it is said by members of his family that many of his characters and situations were based upon actual persons and incidents." This may underscore the comments of an anonymous reviewer of *Ranns & Ballads:* " . . . he had little 'bookishness' in him. But the broad pages of life had no more eager student. One might say that he had a passion for humanity, for patient observation, for delving beneath the crust of character for the well-springs of action." By the same token one might argue that, his work tied closely to transcription of actuality, he had not a triumphantly out-and-out inventive imagination, or at least not one which was consistently operative. Happily, in numerous instances, the result in his case transcends the apparent measure of talent behind it; less happily, the obsessive urge to recast as drama whatever he could sometimes led him astray. For no intensely and *rightly* conceived statement in art is, without injury to its integrity, to be deliberately recarved to fit a mold other than the one it originally assumed: a true play is one first conceived and driven into expression *as* a play. Those short stories of O'Kelly's successfully transformed into plays were, to begin with, not inevitably short stories or finished artistic entities.

VERSE

O'Kelly has been quoted by L. H. Victory as saying, "I think that the less a man knows about the theories of the metrists, the more he is likely to write good poetry." Whether or not the comment has in it an element of self-defense, or any truth whatsoever, it could hardly be supported by O'Kelly's verse, collected or uncollected. For this is, both qualitatively and quantitatively, his least-impressive contribution, so that no one need regret that the publisher never implemented his statement in *Ranns & Ballads,* O'Kelly's one book in its category: "We hope before long to publish a collected edition in which some unpublished and many well-known poems will be included." Seumas O'Sullivan's opinion that O'Kelly was "a great poet"—*i.e.,* in verse—was merely a friendly delusion.

What O'Kelly calls his "Connacht Peep Show" comprises only twenty-seven pieces, nine of which are grouped under the general title of "The Lazy Wall" (mainly a presentation of country characters, though the wall is a seaside one in Salthill, Galway). One of the poems, "The Bard on the Bodach," is a mild curse, reprinted from O'Kelly's broadside; another, "The Shanachie Tells Another Story," had been published in *Aftermath of Easter Week.* By the third poem, "The Tinker," one becomes aware of flawed expertness in handling rhythm and accent—and awareness recurs in reading some subsequent pieces ("Patsy Na Mallacht," "The Tram Horse," "A Pinch of Snuff," "The Spinner," "Mad Sarah"). In the end one has also been jarred by bits of imperfect rhyme stumbling into assonance (*primly / chimney; wine / fire; shaft / cast*) and concludes that, since it is in general technically sophisticated, the book is in spots a bit too casual for even the free-swinging ballad tradition it recalls.

Basically, it is a fictionist's book of people, O'Kelly's

primary interest: shearer, tinker, fisherman, thatcher, and the like. Only once, in the author's speaking of a girl's hair as "like corn" ("The Widower"), does another poet come insistently to mind—however recognizable a general, vague association with the Colum type—as one recalls the "yellow like ripe corn" of Rossetti's *Blessed Damozel*. (O'Kelly had made earlier, and parallel, use of the simile in "the colour of ripened corn," in "The Return of Thade Furey," as also in "The Story of a Spell"—both in *By the Stream of Killmeen*.) Most of its best pieces—"The Ballad of the Twelve Marys," a gruesome record of the working-out of a curse; "A Claddagh Man's Story"; "Mad Sarah"; "The Spinner"; "The Little Branch," of a child stolen by the *sheeóg*—are tragic. But difficult life is not bemoaned: is on occasion presented with a delightful touch of fancy, as in "The Thatcher."

What appeals especially is a *concerned* vitality. Perhaps, like Synge's, the verses are mainly chips from a workshop; but the workshop, again like Synge's, was that of a man who said yea to life—a man, however, whose finest poetry is in his prose tales, especially in his better short stories and *novelle,* as Synge's is in the plays.

What may have been lost in the mostly vanished "Ballad of Sheela Gaul" is a sorry rumination. As things stand, it may well be that O'Kelly's most charming single lyric is the untitled shepherd's song in "The Gray Lake;" at least, he never surpassed its concluding lines: "Dear lady, I'd herd the wild swans in the skies / If they knew of lake water as blue as your eyes!"

DRAMA

The plays are, characteristically, a rather mixed bag, though their author was a natural dramatist, as the rich and lively dialogue of his short stories would be enough to suggest. Even so, Malone seems entirely just in counting the one-act comedies "very much superior" to many produced by the Abbey group, which passed them by except for *Meadowsweet*—and indeed seems to have been careful never to risk overvaluing O'Kelly.

Of the nine (counting the supposed collaboration, *Lustre*) extant, and published, plays, six (*The Matchmakers, The Home-Coming, The Stranger, Driftwood, Meadowsweet, Lustre*) are one-acters; *The Shuiler's Child* is a two-acter; and *The Bribe* and *The Parnellite* are three-acters. Of these, *The Stranger* (a rewritten version of the apparently lost *The Flame on the Hearth*), *The Home-Coming*, and *The Parnellite* (most ambitious of the three) are—overtly or covertly—essentially patriotic propaganda, certainly effective as such, though containing nothing so exalted in kind as, say, the closing touch of *Cathleen Ni Houlihan*, whether that touch originated with Yeats or—as the latter appears to have claimed—with Griffith. And *Driftwood* is clearly second-rate, however successful in production.

The propaganda is very neatly turned in *The Stranger*, in which the unwilling Peter Williams is forced temporarily to protect Michael Dwyer, the notable Wicklow insurgent of the 1798 rebellion, as his wife's price for retaining her and their child. Nevertheless, and aside from the question of whether the dialogue truly suggests the speech of Wicklow, Dwyer's parting declaration that the "man without a country is always a weak man" has a somewhat histrionic ring, whatever one's sympathies. This play lacks the poetic undertones (as when Mrs. Ford remarks that "every sound that goes on the wind is not lost to the dead") of *The Home-Coming,* which O'Kelly called "an attempt to express in the character of Mrs. Ford the eternal peasant in an hour of agrarian triumph," though he may have been recognizing its slightness when he labeled it a "curtain-raiser." For slight in every way it is, this record of intermittently befuddled old Mrs. Ford's ultimate return with her son to the west-of-Ireland farmhouse from which they had been evicted in punishment for her now-dead husband's having led a peasant rising; and the widow's "Ireland herself will rise by the power of her own will" has again the accent of planted oratory. But there is something heart-warming in the neighbors' welcoming back the Fords by plowing their land, as well as in the unabated pride of Mrs. Ford in her dead husband.

The Parnellite, remembered as very popular with amateur dramatic companies, at least puts the Parnell-Gladstone impasse wryly into a nutshell:

Ellen:—Well, could you tell me what it's all about . . .?
Lila:—Yes, I could. Do you see this coloured cartoon?
Ellen:—I do.
Lila:—There's Gladstone for England; there's Parnell for Ireland. Here we have a row of land Acts on a shelf and there is a Home Rule bill on a bench between them.
Ellen:—What? That shapeless sawdust doll?
Lila:—Yes. They're going to stitch her up and when they

pass her through parliament she's supposed to walk
out a lovely live creature. When they have her half
robed Gladstone ups and says to Parnell, "You're
not a respectably married man like me. I was never
in a divorce court like you. So I won't dress any
more Irish dolls with you in my house. My heart
bleeds for Ireland but my conscience is Noncon-
formist."

Ellen:—I see, faith. Well?

Lila:—When some of the Irish people hear that they say,
"We'll have to unfrock Parnell and send somebody
else to thread the needles for Gladstone." And Parnell ups and says, "I'm your ordained man. That
doll is mine, not his. I have a mind to make her
what nobody else on earth can make her, the live-
liest toy that a nation ever played with." So others
of the Irish people when they hear that say, "We'll
stick to our own good man. Let Parnell at Gladstone
now and he'll make him finish that doll or else
eat her sawdust" . . . And that's the whole case,
Ellen: the rest is all a man's disease, parliamentary
liver, God help us!

The action of the play covers the nine years following
its opening in 1881, when Stephen O'Moore, tenant of
a west-of-Ireland farmhouse, insists on honoring Parnell's Land-League manifesto against paying rent on
holdings until the people are given their constitutional
rights. For resisting the Crown forces, Stephen—who has
had only doubtful intermittent support from his brother
Gerald, his sister Lila, and his tacitly betrothed Ellen,
sister of Father Barrett—is given eighteen months at
hard labor after a mock trial under a stupid judge. (The
prosecutor is Stephen's landlord's personal solicitor!)
In 1890, Stephen, then living in a hut and working as
a hired farmhand, finds people turning against Parnell—

and consequently him—because of the O'Shea divorce action; and in the perhaps over-protracted end, is forsaken by all and stoned to death by a risen populace.

Though essentially the exploitation of Parnellite propaganda, this ambitious play has much moving content and reveals O'Kelly clearly as a Roman Catholic who in the midst of political and religious bigotry insisted on thinking for himself. The real question seems to be one of pace, related to that of adequate dramatic condensation—frequently O'Kelly's albatross except in the remarkable short stories. Further, the dialogue seems far less deliberately Irish in colloquial quality than usual—and perhaps to a corresponding degree less rich in poetic content. Nor are the characters sharply individualized. Father Barrett is just the conventional parish priest; Stephen himself is merely a type of inflexible Parnellite; Ellen is nothing more than a vaguely vacillating girl; the agents of British "justice" (not least the stupid presiding officer, Major Heatherley) are almost caricatures in the light of satiric presentation; and so on. In the end, one agrees with Malone (*The Irish Drama*, p. 197) that the play is "effective rather than thrilling."

The least satisfactory of O'Kelly's remaining plays seems to me to be *Driftwood*, a mildly interesting piece labeled a "comedy," though its spirit seems less clearly comic than weakly sardonic. Herein the dialogue centers around a play, "Driftwood," just written by George Drake (himself a self-centered bit of wooden conceit) — an Ibsenesque piece about a woman who is leaving her husband after ten years of marriage to become "drift-

wood." Mrs. Drake, an actress, questions the psychology
and obviously unnatural dialogue of the script she is
reading with her husband while they await Maurice
Hamlyn, who is to be cast as the hero. Hamlyn (whose
name seems significant) stays only briefly after arrival,
approves the play, but—keyed up by a current love affair—leaves without rehearsing after the arrival of
Kendal Nugent, a critic, who damns "Driftwood" as
"glorified Punch and Judy" untrue to life—only to have
his ex-wife appear and reveal to Mrs. Drake that after
ten years of married life she has left Nugent because of
his affair with a waitress.

Too patently managed coincidence weakened by in-
exact parallelism between Drake's heroine and Mrs.
Nugent may be what lames the play, to whose essential
progress Hamlyn seems quite unnecessary. The sardonic
humor lies in the fact that Mrs. Nugent does represent
the sort of driftwood her ex-husband (perhaps in fear of
eventual personal publicity) had claimed to be unlife-
like, and one motivated by a psychology Mrs. Drake had
counted doubtful.

The supposed collaboration (perhaps mainly with
reference to plot, since the dialogue seems unadulter-
ated O'Kelly?) *Lustre,* which may here be given transi-
tional comment between remarks on the propagandistic
and intrinsically less interesting plays and reflections on
those I think more likely to endure, has perhaps had
anything but the attention it deserves. Not by any means
an overwhelming achievement, it is yet an effective
brief tragedy turning on the behavior of the brutalized
Jimmy Donnellan, last of the widowed Cauth's children,

after coming home on "sick furlough" from the Connacht Rangers to the detested west-of-Ireland cabin where he was spawned. In effect, Jimmy murders his mother after trying to steal the pieces of lustre—center of all her cherished memories—which she has refused to sell, and which, after she has caught him in his would-be theft, he cruelly smashes.

The play has only four characters, of whom the gentle and broken Cauth is the most memorable; but there is reasonable psychology in its revelation of how the innocently well-meaning mother has sown revolt in her favorite child through overprotecting and babying him. And somehow there was avoided the maudlin sentimentalism to which the very character of the situation might well have been conducive.

Turning to O'Kelly's least debatable plays, we find as earliest *The Matchmakers,* one of his two successful transformations out of short-story form, a good piece of play-cobbling. Herein each of two rival matchmakers plans to hoodwink the other. Larry Dolan hides with a cloak his niece Mary's lack of a right hand, while Tom O'Connor conceals with a greatcoat his brother Sean's bandy legs, each hoping the deception will not be exposed before the marriage agreement is signed and witnessed. But the intended witness, Kate Mulvany—having, to prevent "the playing off of a decent man on a decent girl," secretly informed the couple of the planned deception and happily found the defects mutually acceptable—turns the tables on the matchmakers and scares the wits out of them before asserting, "When people cotton to each other like Sean and Mary a leg or an arm here or there makes no great odds." If this longish one-acter imposes any strain on credibility, it is only that of accepting the doubtful grotesquery of concealment involved, though this is perhaps nothing compared, say, with the strain of swallowing Yeats's *Pot of Broth*.

The variously revived *Meadowsweet,* in turn, a satiric piece relating to the Irish "Labourers Act," is a lightly amiable brevity whose "Kiltartan" lingo (the play is laid in the Connacht countryside) happily lacks the exaggeration of Lady Gregory's. Herein Kevin Monahan's plan to plague Luke Tierney, his rival in landowning, backfires when it appears that the Rural Council has appropriated an acre of his own best land instead of Luke's on which to build the latter's employee, Johnny Claffey, a house, and when Kevin's servant Maria, finding that all is conditional upon Johnny's marriage, decides to take this homely and previously rejected suitor after all! Not least amusing here is the satiric innuendo about the handling of taxpayers' money; not least charming is Johnny's turn of phrase, which has often the color of Irish folk poetry upon it. And the piece ends delightfully with Maria wheeling the now-in-charge Claffey to "the hill of Lacken to . . . scent the meadowsweet." Of course, as a comedy of situation purely, the play is close to farce. It is another piece evolved out of a short story.

Entertaining brevities aside, O'Kelly's real claim to significance as a dramatist is established by *The Shuiler's Child* and *The Bribe,* both rightly praised by Malone. In the former, chance brings the shuiler Moll Woods to

Kilbeg and the house of Andy and Nannie O'Hea, who are rearing Moll's child, Phil, left in a workhouse by his mother after her husband has absconded. An officious lady inspector to the Local Government Board then appears and intimates that she will (really quite unjustly) have Phil, in whose mother the maternal instinct has reawakened, transferred to other foster parents. Later, Moll, really motivated by a desire for authority to assure Phil to the O'Heas, regains charge of him on a legal technicality. But she is in the end arrested for her early desertion of the child and leaves prophesying for herself a future of the roads and dissolution.

This is a heartbreaking play, with every character except the child (in whose case development is not necessary) a distinct personality. And the natural poetry of the dialogue is unforced and qualitatively colloquial, with such glosses of life as Officer O'Halloran's " . . . it's a poor heart that never knows a merry mood," "The man that is always thinking of rain never feels a dry skin," "People that turn their backs to the light of the moon soon grow blind in the sun." Of course, Moll, vacillating in her desire to regain her child but in the end acting for his good, is the most sympathetic character; and it is not easy to forget her lament when she is initially rebuffed by the child: "No, he wouldn't come near the Shuiler. I'm of no more account now than a broken mist on the hill."

Mr. J. B. McGuire, with the happy assurance of the doctoral candidate, disparages this play in "Realism in Irish Drama" as a "dated" thing in which O'Kelly permits "the propaganda [save the mark!] to swamp the drama"; and Vivian Mercier, in his doctoral thesis, counts it, strangely, "rather disappointing reading." Malone (*Dublin Magazine,* July–September 1930) seems nearer justice in saying it "should come as near immortality as can be achieved"; certainly it is the real evidence supporting his further opinion (cf. "The Decline of the Irish Drama") that O'Kelly, had he lived, "might have rivalled Synge in the tragic intensity of his work."

Character is equally convincing in *The Bribe,* another potent tragedy. Herein the stupid Dr. Jack O'Connor is in competition with the brilliant Dr. Luke Diamond, son of a poor widow and shopkeeper, for appointment to the post of dispensary doctor in Garrymore, from which O'Connor's father is retiring. The elder O'Connor is bribing board members for votes, but is initially unsuccessful with John Kirwan, who has promised Luke to abstain from voting, thus leaving him to win, expectedly, by one vote, which, however, turns out also to have been bought. Meanwhile, O'Connor has assured the shamed Kirwan's breaking the tie in his son's favor by leaving a check for £80 to redeem a mortgage on their land and stock which Kirwan's wife has secretly arranged with a "gombeen man"—a friend of O'Connor's—to meet a business account. So Luke loses, but accepts as honest Kirwan's explanation that he had changed his mind.

In the ironic, and powerful, end, the young Dr. O'Connor admits himself unable to save the pregnant and critically ill wife of Kirwan and calls for Luke—then preparing to leave for Australia—too late to save her: a judgment on Kirwan in Luke's embittered mother's view. Luke himself, queried, tells Kirwan he could not have saved the baby: "But the mother's life—don't press the question, John."

O'Kelly had a deeply sympathetic view of human nature, and even the bribing old Dr. O'Connor is so presented that the light is true yet leaves him understandable as a worried father. Indeed, every character rings clear, with the life-hardened, self-sacrificing Mrs. Diamond and Kirwan's gentle sister, Mary (Luke's original inspiration, though sadly too old to be his love), finally the most deeply moving figures. Ironically enough, Luke to the end naïvely believes Kirwan honest; and the tragic third act carries almost unbearable tension. Or so it seems to me; Ernest Boyd (*The Contemporary Drama of Ireland,* p. 153) feels "The *dénouement* is rather obvious, but it is the only comparatively weak point in the play, which excels in the sober veracity of its uncompromising analysis of provincial manners, political and social."

For myself, I must count the two plays just considered only a pace or two behind the finest products of the Irish Renaissance, even though their author is brilliantly ignored by Una Ellis-Fermor and Peter Kavanagh, and merely named by Murray in the Robinson-edited *Irish Theatre.* Malone sees here, and elsewhere, an impress of Ibsen (in the concern with contemporary problems); and one recalls O'Kelly's confession to Mary Walker that Ibsen set him off on *The Shuiler's Child.* But certainly one sees no real imitation, no Ibsenesque dourness; and one may feel that O'Kelly has, speaking through George

Drake, the dramatist in *Driftwood,* made the rational comment: "There is nothing wrong with Ibsen as Ibsen, but there is something wrong and something pervert about the bogey that men . . . try to make of his genius."

Malone is, on the other hand, unarguable in his feeling that O'Kelly's comedies are not up to his tragedies; and he is only in the case of a few exceptions not irrefutable in his assertion (*The Irish Drama,* p. 198), "In technique and dramatic power he is the equal of any English-writing dramatist of the contemporary theatre." Of course, O'Kelly is best when unconcerned with overt propaganda; and if he lacks, say, Synge's highest moments of exaltation, grotesque humor, and sustained power, he also lacks the artificial, though charming, language in which all this is webbed: if he has not Yeats's agony of concentrated poetic statement, he does have constantly a humane element which is not always apparent in the greater man.

PROSE FICTION

Novels

O'Kelly's two published novels are works that stand in sharp contrast with each other. Clearly—as reexamination confirms—the posthumously published *Wet Clay* is anything but exceptional tale-telling. Its clichés and pictures of a peasantry presented with sentimentality and a touch of melodrama, its assumption of a detailed knowledge on the part of the reader of the Irish Land War and its confused aftermath, its rather plodding pace, and its utterly absurd efforts at suggesting the speech of an Irish-American born and reared in New York (at least a semi-intellectual, with training in literature and music) by such phrases as "I don't quite reckon you," "I guess I'll hoof it," ". . . let's have a bit of a hippo," "Oh, Aunt Sara, I say!", and the like *ad nauseam* combine to make an O'Kelly enthusiast marvel at what bathos honest ability can sometimes plumb.

Brendan Nilan comes to mend his health, and hopefully to become a farmer, to the holdings of his near relatives at Clonlea, about twelve miles from Ballyrea (which, with its "grey lake" and cathedral, is obviously Loughrea once more) and within hilltop sight of the Bay of Galway. Almost immediately he meets by the grey lake Ellen Noonan (destined to become a nun) and Martha Lee (his tragic fixation). Heartily welcomed by his aunt, grandmother, and cousin Mark Cusack, he is from the beginning resented and insultingly treated by his boorish other cousin, Luke, a potential alcoholic.

Details of the straggling story are hardly necessary here. Enough to say that the uncouth Luke marries—incredibly—the sensitive but unstable Martha, and Brendan fights down his own desire for the girl until he can no longer contain himself. This point is reached when—in mock Roman Catholic fashion, though she seems only nominally religious—she returns to Luke after temporarily leaving him because of his brutality. After a feverish confession of his passion, to which she feels no reciprocal response, Brendan struggles with, and kisses, her. Rewarded by a hurled chair, he departs. Shortly afterward, the drunken Luke is temporarily prevented by a servant from shooting him, though he *is* shot and killed when the gun goes off during an ensuing struggle for its possession. Meanwhile there has been much gabbling, *passim*, about the character and troubles of the tenant farmers finally come into their own.

As is intimated in the biographical sketch, the enthusiasm of Irish reviewers of this book was amazing; yet if it were what Gwynn calls it—"one of the best among modern Irish novels"—the Irish novel would be in a sorry plight indeed. Nor are the comparisons with Hardy justified; there is a difference between coincidence and card-stacking. We are to believe that Martha, a talented musician, marries the boor Luke to escape threatened apprenticeship in millinery, with Brendan, better than her match in taste and training, as readily available: marries him, endures his drunken brutality and uncouthness, and returns after her breakaway on the suasion of a nun whose religious impulses she has more than once disparaged! But she is not the only unconvincing figure. We are, indeed, presented with a large assortment of characters of whom only one, the grandmother, has the fibre to emerge an interesting individual. And we are given all this in a lamely sprawling narrative whose main value may lie in its general projection of a thoroughly discouraging rural society and landscape. In the end, one concludes that the title from Omar Khayyám (strange what a steady appeal the *Rubáiyát* had for the unrebellious Christian O'Kelly!) was well chosen on more grounds than one. And when we are told that it is the American "national weakness to deliver a brief lecture" (and feel, not for the first

time, that O'Kelly seemed to nurture a curious resent-
ment toward America) , we are likely to reflect that this
novel is itself in a sense little more than a moral lecture
—unfortunately not brief.

This said, it should be added that the pallid Brendan
is a character whose ascribed philosophy of life contains
an element, as I have said elsewhere, which seemingly
was also a part of O'Kelly's: "an undercurrent of humour that amounted, despite its occasional irony, to
almost a charity." And one suspects that O'Kelly is also
speaking for himself when he has Brendan write to
Mark: "I was . . . so susceptible to the life about me
that the light could not fade in the hills but that I was
conscious of it and alive to the mystery and hidden
things it expressed." For here are suggested both the
sensitivity and the sympathy which help explain O'Kelly
at his best.

The Lady of Deerpark (ironically enough, issued only
from London, and related, as we have been reminded,
to an early short story) is another matter. Laid in the
Kilbeg countryside (Loughrea area, Co. Galway) , this
is the tragic story of Mary Heffernan, a lovely woman
with "the eyes of a child and the restraint of a seer,"
recorded by Paul Jennings, son and successor to the
former agent of the Heffernan family. Mary returns to
dilapidated Deerpark the night of her dissolute brother's
suicide and remains uneasily immured there with a
woman servant until word from Australia brings news
that she is heir to the entire estate of her wealthy
nephew George, her brother's only son. Thereafter begins the rejuvenation of Deerpark—and Mary's subtle

wooing of Paul, whose heart has already been given to the lovely Betty Carolan, a miller's daughter (a weakly limned figure).

Presently the heartbroken Mary accedes to the forced attentions of the subtly vulgar racehorse-breeder "Kish" Massy, described as in youth "a skillful thrower of bowls on the roads, a game not yet quite abandoned in rural Ireland, possibly because it is illegal." Paul is amazed, but can not declare a love he does not feel; and presently Mary, desirous of children, marries Kish. Of course, the latter, denied control of Mary's fortune, eventually descends to physical abuse; when his wife refuses to die, he takes off for America (and a previous inamorata), presently cabling his intention to file for divorce naming Paul as co-respondent and paramour. Shocked, Mary gives birth prematurely and dies an hour before her child.

Kish returns from New York with a new wife and a Yankee lawyer father-in-law—and is within a few years financially "milked" by the latter, while the former elopes with Kish's unpalatable friend Lord Elmtree. Kish, in youth given to climbing, suffers delirium tremens before escaping from constraint with the drunken assertion that he would climb "up an elm tree if it was to cost him his life": a bit of overcontrivance which mars the novel but furnishes bones for the ever-hungry hounds of symbol—though unhappily in this case a rather doubtfully functional symbol rooted in a pun. Eventually Kish is found, grotesquely choked and suspended by a nightshirt from a crane overhanging the Heffernan marble quarries. (Malone, quoting an anonymous commentator, describes this scene as " 'a monstrous parody on a hooked fish.' ")

If this is not a work with the epic impact of a *Wind from the North* or the whimsical brilliance of a *Demi-Gods,* and it isn't, neither is it one with the soporific meanderings of an *Héloïse and Abélard,* the weary psychologizing of certain more-popular O'Flaherty exhibits, or the academically exalted irrationality of a *Finnegans Wake.* True, it has that slow, protracted, and overly contrived ending just remarked; and it might conceivably have benefited from better structural balancing of its elements. Against weakness suggested, however, may be placed real achievement in character-delineation (from which Kish, Mary, and Mary's friend Lady Newell emerge as most clearly presented), felicities such as "I left with the elation which one might carry from the house of a poet," vignettes such as that of the "old man ... with a mouth like a vacant potato-pit," and passages of genuine power—none better than the one describing Paul's overhearing of the tragic and abandoned harp-music into which Mary plunges after he has left her in no further doubt of his inability to respond to her love:

> Suddenly the chords of the harp in an amazingly strong, harsh stroke came crashing down the corridor outside. It seemed to tear through the silent house, something volcanic in its sudden escape. I had no idea that a harp could gather such strength in its penetrating strains. It seemed to leap at me like a living thing as I sat on the chair and it gripped me there. I could not move. I could scarcely breathe. I was intensely responsive to the emotion, for although I play no instrument I am unusually sensitive to the influence of music; this, again, gave me some nearness to Miss Heffernan, who was, I felt now more than

ever, a daughter of Jubal, her soul instinctively seeking self-expression through the harp. The music that now held me so powerfully was not any conventional composition, and at first seemed not even a definite or connected composition. It was ugly, terrible, the notes sharp, the discords painful, but as it tore its way along I felt it aimed at something and expressed something. And above the harsh discords there struck out, thin and sharp, a *motif* that surely had its source in some folk tune, elemental and disturbing. And there was a certain crude rhythm in the tearing discords, the notes most powerful in their harshness, urged on as it were by some velocity that was vindictive, and above the brutal jargon of sound was that weird, very definite *motif*, shrilling up over it all, ironic and terrible. I felt moved, shaken, almost exhausted by this experience, and like a flash the thought went across my mind that all of emotion and hope and desire and despair that lay behind the platitudes Miss Heffernan had dropped in her boudoir was now speaking, clear and unmistakable, in this rush of mad sound. It did not come on any scale of harmony and yet with terribly flexible and unashamed meaning, the child of an inspiration that was itself too savage to obey a form, too crude to step to a technique.

I clutched the arms of my chair and said, "This is the music of something lost, this is a thing of hysteria and madness!" And as I listened I felt that in no way could this music be interpreted except, perhaps, by the dance of a woman who would have in her body and her limbs the hysteria and the madness, in her face and her gestures the horror of a lost soul. And instantly there came to my mind the memory of a scene witnessed on a little yellow road in Connemara, a scene that had brought me nightmares in the years gone by. A young tinker woman, comely and courageous in the daring beauty of her kind, wearing a gay petticoat of red and white stripes, a blue bodice, her rich brown hair tumbling about her shoulders, danced in her bare feet on the road, beating up the dust, something fantastic and insane in her movements. She danced in the bright sun of a summer day and she kept her face, ghastly pale, to the sun, her upper white teeth showing through the blue line of her lips. She had, I knew at once, danced up and down the road, her eyes half closed, for a longer time than a normal physical reserve would allow, and she would go on dancing, seeing nothing, paying attention to nothing, until she fell in a swoon in the yellow dust of the lonely mountain road. And as I went by that dancing mad woman, I saw under a heeled-up cart in the ditch the dead body of a young man, lying stark on his back, her husband or her lover, but one who had died of love. She was dancing up and down by the side of the cart under which he lay dead, and this music which now had broken forth in Deerpark was such music as the limbs of that young tinker woman might have interpreted, for the hysteria and the madness were in them. And it was such music as might have swept the seas and the nations and all time, and found its votaries. It was to music such as this that the limbs of Electra might have moved before the Eastern palace at the hour Orestes struck the blow which brought down the traitor mother queen, Clytemnestra. It was fit measure for the movements of Salome when she danced before the throne of Herod bearing on a dish the head of John the Baptist.

"God!" I cried, "this is the music of a soul writhing under the sense of damnation!" It stopped quite suddenly, as if from exhaustion, on a bar that sounded like a gash.

Perhaps this passage may suggest why Forrest Reid, in his review of *The Golden Barque,* counted *The Lady of Deerpark,* to its time, "probably the best novel . . . out of Ireland"; why Seumas O'Sullivan, to whom it was dedicated, refers to it in *Essays and Recollections* as one which "with all its faults," has "elements of greatness in it." Never, says Malone, in his general essay on O'Kelly, "was story of a 'Big House' told with such power as in the section of this novel entitled 'After the Marriage.' " Further, it is O'Kelly's closest approximation of a great love story: "approximation" because this author did not have it in him to write a triumphantly great love story; he could never have imagined a Rita or even a Eustacia Vye, though possibly a Marty South. In any event, however, I think it suggestive of the sort of story in which Emily Brontë might have taken sympathetic pleasure— and that is intended as a reflection implying no mean praise.

Edain (cf. the ancient *Courtship of Etain*), O'Kelly's other book-length romance, seems to be extant only in fragmentary portions. We know (see §C, 1, Bibliography, below) that the original manuscript ran to 273 pages, since the last two are included in some 80 pages preserved; and that the first six chapters alone were posthumously published. The manuscript (of which one estimates from 100 to 120 pages to be missing) suggests, by virtue of errors in spelling and in the handling of antique forms ("of the reason thou struck," "I knowest now I hath found," etc.), early work; yet the pace is curiously that of a practiced, or at least "natural," storyteller—and the theme, seemingly of a wicked druid's eventually foiled machinations to possess the wife of King Eochaidth (*sic:* Eochaid?), is colorful and interesting (in one sequence Edain and a servant are captured and taken to King Ailiol, of Connacht, about to war on Eochaidth). In short, this tale (obviously sheer invention using some characters from recorded story and perhaps a little suggestive of Scott's type of coloration) seems a real loss. What it might have been with careful technical editing and full presentation is at present one of the futilities associated with pondering O'Kelly's history.

Short Stories and *Novelle*

O'Kelly's most luminous and poetic work is indubitably to be found in his shorter fiction, of which the notable collections are *Waysiders, The Golden Barque and The Weaver's Grave,* and *Hillsiders.* From these books could be excluded relatively few tales whose loss to literature would not be a sorry one. And that is no small assertion. But let us look at the short stories and *novelle* in the large, beginning with O'Kelly's first collection, *By the Stream of Killmeen,* without pretending any special significance as to development suggested by chronological progression. The truth is that we know next to nothing about actual dates of writing, and that both *Waysiders* and *The Golden Barque* . . . mingle early with late work, whereas *Hillsiders* contains only early tales, excellent volume though it be.

As the *Leinster Leader* summarized, *By the Stream of Killmeen* concerns "matchmaking, emigration, eviction; the disheartening loneliness of a country laid waste," though O'Kelly "preserves the idyllic temper throughout." But despite the approving excitement of Irish reviewers, the book has not a single memorable piece in it, even though it may be granted a casual type of readability. One notes quickly its direct or implied moralizing; its observational accuracy with respect to flora; its gentle, half-sentimental tone. And one reflects that one or two pieces are essentially essays rather than stories: *e.g.,* "The Story of a Spell," involving a bit of romantically historical rumination. But there is nothing to urge a rereading.

The Leprechaun of Killmeen, a shocking example of

the results of bad proofreading, is, in turn, really a frame arrangement of two groups of stories (three to each group), though the episodes are related. Herein a favorite character of O'Kelly's, the shanachie "Oul' Tom Kelleher," tells his tales—verbosely—to a group of boys who have been helping Ned Darmody in his haying.

We learn how a leprechaun had been transformed and sent into the world by the Queen of the Fairies, who was opposed to his marrying her daughter, and doomed to remain until he had hidden enough crocks of gold to match Croagh Patrick in piled height. In the first three tales the leprechaun tricks Tom out of his crock of gold after being caught; in the second, he escapes the pursuing countryside on the back of a bull after bargaining for a crutch with old Thade Casey, whom he enriches with a crock of gold. In consequence, the leprechaun is finally able to return to Tir na nOg (*Land of the Young*), become a "big man" there, and marry his princess. The invention herein exhibited is certainly of the garden variety; the telling is oppressive with too much dialectal coyness of the "Sure 'twas moidhered me head was entirely" variety. In brief, the book is a bore assembled from some of O'Kelly's earlier efforts at fiction-writing.

"At the Burning of the Sod," it may here be remarked, is a set of six tales sequential to those of *The Leprechaun of Killmeen*. Herein, at the instance of his hearers, Tom Kelleher admits that the leprechaun had not permanently disappeared on the back of a bull, but had returned and "cuckooed" at him from a hollow tree.

Thereafter he tells of the capture of the leprechaun by his wife, of the leprechaun's escape while enforcedly leading the Kellehers into the Malleystown caves, of a chase through a ruined castle and by log-raft down a river toward Galway Bay (with near-drowning), of re-capture by Mrs. Kelleher, and of the leprechaun's ulti-mate vanishing after identifying the real "good red gold" as the tillable soil of Ireland. There is less here of the coyly dialectal than in the earlier leprechaun tales (as if O'Kelly realized he had overdone it there), with the explanation that Tom had reduced the "full flavour" of his speech because he was addressing "a more grown audience" before the sod fire at night. O'Kelly achieves more artistry and suspense here than in the earlier series, especially in "The Caves," but the whole business un-fortunately resolves itself into a sociological moraliza-tion. Gold of a finer carat than the leprechaun ever secreted or revealed appeared in the three major collec-tions.

The latest of these in date of publication, *Hillsiders*, comprises matter first issued serially in 1909. It includes six tales, the first three of which might, without tre-mendous manipulation, have been amalgamated into a novel.

Best of all in *Hillsiders* would seem to be "The Miracle of the Tea," "Nan Hogan's House," and "The Elks" (a powerful story despite a slightly rushed and sentimental ending and a tiresomely repetitious use of the phrase "the little mother": certainly not the "flimsy" tale it has been labeled). But all the narratives are very readable (and some, again, disgracefully proofread and

in need of editing) , from the account of the indomitable
char Hannah, who links the opening and the second
stories, through the three tales just singled out, to the
concluding revelation of Pa Cloone, a great liar, scared
grey by a supposed "apparition" (really a brooding
goose lodged under his bed). Action, incidentally, is
here frequently a result of village gossip and its expan-
sion through avid repetition (one recalls Lady Gregory);
but in the end one has a very friendly feeling for
"Kilbeg" and its environs, though it is—save for a few
exceptions—the group rather than the individual that
impresses most.

Among the exceptions must be included the pathetic
Winnie O'Carroll, whose belief in contemporary mir-
acles suffers when a packet of tea she has found in her
husband's cart and innocently used becomes the spark
igniting great and unjust suspicions in Kilbeg until she
secretly replaces it with one of greater size, slipped
through the window of the intended recipient of the
original packet! Another is the bitter-tongued and
crippled widow Nan Hogan, whose leg "weakness"
eventually yields to sheer determination and proves unable to keep her in the poorhouse hospital; and a third
is assuredly Fardy Lalor, whose "quiet eyes . . . somehow
suggested the sea and held in their depths the making of
storms," and whose pugnacious childhood opened on a
maturity rendered heroic by his rescue of a once-hated
rival in love from the deadly reef know as "The Elks."

Waysiders, in turn, is a book of less-even accomplishment than *Hillsiders,* though it sometimes suggests
greater maturity and contains several of O'Kelly's finest

achievements, for the sake of which we may abide the weaker ones: "Both Sides of the Pond," "A Wayside Burial," and "The Rector." One piece is a reprinting of the one-act play *The Home-Coming,* which has had earlier comment; two—"The White Goat" and "The Sick Call"—fall within O'Kelly's middle range. In the former, a herd kills his white goat out of pity after it has been senselessly and fatally abused by drunken laborers, and then worries about punishment for having violated the course of nature, inevitably to be predicted though that was; in the latter, the author, in the role of Mass-server in a monastery, accompanies the Spanish friar who, as a supposedly healing agent, answers a call to "raise his holy hands over Kevin Hooban." The friar prays over this young *fideóg* (flute) -player, and the sick man is released from the imagined grip of "the Good People." There is little action, but a surprising sense of drama is evoked in the picture of the anxious peasants grouped outside Kevin's cabin; the clichés ("a breath of wind"; "silence . . . reigned," though long overdue for dethronement; etc.) , happily, can not harm the good passages (*e.g.,* "The whole landscape had swooned away into a dark, vague chaos") .

In "Both Sides of the Pond," after a local girl leaves for Australia, the young turf-cutter Denis Donohoe by implication leaves his primitive Connacht bog cabin— and presumably his mother—for America, thus achieving his cynical stance as a singer in a Broadway honky-tonk and what a female half-caste there approves as " 'one of the boys.' " O'Kelly's emigrants generally come to no good in America, and this story amounts to just one more chunk of sentimentalized mush. The other two weak pieces can hardly be called stories. "The Rector" is merely a mildly satiric bit on a dour Protestant rector in Connacht, with just a hint of submerged propaganda in it; "A Wayside Burial" (in which O'Kelly calls himself "the eternal observer") presents the author in attendance on a priest hurrying to the workhouse graveyard to bury Martin Quirke, broken with his brother " 'under the Plan of Campaign—the time of the evictions,' " fighting " 'landlordism' "—and gives him an excuse to meditate on other dead or vanished paupers as well.

The notable stories in *Waysiders* are unarguably "The Can with the Diamond Notch," "The Shoemaker," "The Gray Lake," and "The Building." Of these, the first—briefly, an account of how the country merchant Festus Clasby is thoroughly "taken" by "Mac-an-Ward, the Son of the Bard" and a group of fellow tinkers—is as delightful as anything O'Kelly ever wrote; "The Shoemaker" recounts a cobbler's entertaining the boy Padna with charming tall tales, concluded with a remarkable satire on the sad state of the Irish in a town cursed with a *good* landlord; and "The Building" presents the tragedy of Martin Cosgrave, who sacrifices everything to build on a hill a large limestone house in anticipation of the return from America of his fiancée Rose Dempsey. The unworthy Rose (obviously also "gone wrong" in America) jilts him, and the broken Martin has to return to the cabin and the life of the soil —but does so without moaning.

It is "The Gray Lake," in the last analysis, which perhaps leaves the most persistent impression. Like "The Can with the Diamond Notch" a short *novella* in length, it is a masterly, and completely beautiful, account of the drowning of a town, now under the lake in reference, by seven water-nymphs released from their enclosed well by a shepherd whose reward is the keeper's daughter. In the description of the rising of the waters—as I have elsewhere attested—is a genuine poetic frenzy channeled into memorable, almost epic, statement: it is particularly hard to forget how "women, turning from the race to the hills, rushed back to meet the oncoming waters with arms outspread and insanity in their wild eyes."

Waysiders alone would have demonstrated O'Kelly's aversion to taking anything at second hand and suggested convincingly that both sight and insight were personal, that his capacity for original figures of speech was matched by that of meeting a dramatic situation as no second-rater could, and that his amused and warm affection for fellow humans was beyond any condescension. And there was corroborative evidence ahead. It lies in *The Golden Barque and The Weaver's Grave.*

The first portion of this title designates a series of six tales—vignettes of a kind—loosely interrelated in that they concern canal boatmen sometime employed on "The Golden Barque." The stories are among O'Kelly's more-accomplished pieces and exploit a reasonable range of interest. Qualitatively as good as any is "Michael and Mary," a gently tragic idyl; most shocking is the depiction of a father's almost incredible brutality presented in "The Derelict"; memorable and diverting in other ways are also the registration of boyish and painful hero-worship (the boy, I have been told, is the young Alphonsus Sweeney) in "Billy the Clown" and the humorous memorialization of the ignorant Martin Coughlan, undeservedly regarded as a "Man with the Gift" (of eloquence).

But it is the *novella* indicated in the second part of the general title which overshadows everything else in this volume—and perhaps everything else O'Kelly ever did. For assuredly *The Weaver's Grave* (on no rational grounds to be called, as it has been—though not for the first time—by Miss Rose, "An Irish Widow of Ephesus") is to be ranked among the world's finest specimens of its category—with O'Connor's *The Holy Door,* Conrad's *Heart of Darkness,* Stephens' *The Feast of Lugnasa,* Galsworthy's *The Apple Tree,* Isak Dinesen's *Ehrengard,* to mention a few others of equivalent, though diverse, qualification. Incidentally, it reminds one that the Irish, contrary to E. Grennan's assertion that the "long short story" was "never followed to any great extent in Ireland," have excelled numerously in the *novella,* as not only the work of O'Connor, O'Kelly, and Stephens, but that of O'Faoláin, Ella Young, and Maurice Walsh, among others, attests.

Subtly humane, quietly poetic in concept, deceptively simple in statement and character-revelation, this picture of two crotchety old fellows, Meehaul Lynskey and Cahir Bowes, sarcastically disputing with each other the correct spot in which the ancient weaver Mortimer Hehir is entitled to be buried while a fresh and proper love begins dawning for his youthful widow (and fourth

wife!) and a gravedigger, is one of the rarities of literature. One reason lies in the dialogue of the ancients, in
which, as O'Hanlon has remarked in *The Capuchin
Annual, 1949,* "almost every sentence is Gaelic in con-
struction." And somehow, without falsification of the
size of what is actually a small, and except for age un-
impressive, burial ground near the eastern end of
Loughrea, O'Kelly leads the reader into an imagined
area that seems physically as extensive as it is historically
significant. All of which makes it the sadder that
O'Kelly's engagement with this story was interrupted by
his own death, leaving some minor technical imperfec-
tions unresolved. But mortality has never more justly
provided excuse for a gently humorous aftermath than
it furnishes here, where the truth of David Morton's
comment is reemphasized: "The life of O'Kelly's people
was dusty and grim—but it was a fiery dust and a pas-
sionate grimness, touched with a kind of nobility, that
made life a beautiful thing." Perhaps, too, this tale
suggests what Darrell Figgis meant when he said, "it
was not his particular excellence to tell a tale . . . it was
his excellence to let the tale tell him"; what Forrest
Reid implied in remarking in *Retrospective Adventures*
that "the effect of his finest stories is infinitely richer
than the sum of their recorded happenings."

The uncollected brief fiction would hardly add to
O'Kelly's stature if assembled into book form, though
some specimens would not diminish it. It includes such
matter as *An Island Eve,* a tale rooted in hypochondria,
superstition, and smuggling, in which the author sets the
stage for tragedy and then manipulates a happy ending;

The Marriage Money, a cleverly plotted bit of common-
place in which two sisters get husbands at the eventual
expense of one of the men (a niggardly Scot) and open
the door to a third marriage; and *The Revenge of
Seaghan Buidhe,* a melodramatic piece of just retribu-
tion among members of a secret political society in
which the president, Seaghan, turns out to be the government "spy" and "traitor" (shot by peelers in the end,
the title being ironic) , but a semi-juvenile performance
with its apparatus of deserted house, crying owls, and
the like. Aside from these, one may name the eight
scattered "Padna" pieces; some fugitive tales adequately
pointed in §C of the Annotated Bibliography; and "At
the Burning of the Sod" (noticed above in connection
with *The Leprechaun of Killmeen*) .

The "Padna" (O'Kelly himself as a boy) sketches are
casually interesting tales of a variety appropriate to popular magazine or newspaper publication: *e.g.,* in "The
Golden Wren" Padna gets a gun for Christmas from an
uncle in America, kills a golden wren on Christmas
morning, and thereafter suffers a nightmare and sharp
remorse; in "Padna at the Play," the boy sneaks into a
play-booth at "Ballyrea" (cf. *Wet Clay*) , sees a performance break up in a husband-wife performers' fight, but
wins free admission to future performances by carrying
porter for another member of the company; and so on.
But certainly there is nothing here gasping for resusci-
tation. The memorable O'Kelly tales remain those collected in *Waysiders, Hillsiders,* and *The Golden Barque
and The Weaver's Grave;* but the cumulation therein
contained would be adequate memorial for any man,

even if unbuttressed by *The Lady of Deerpark* (sadly in need of reprinting) and several splendid plays. Why Ireland remembers the author of these almost exclusively in disregardful association with *The Weaver's Grave* in isolation is one of the perplexing annoyances of literary history.

Forrest Reid, in his essay in *Retrospective Adventures,* has very justly remarked: "O'Kelly was a realist ... But he was not a materialist. He looked at life simply and directly, and there was nothing significant in life from which he turned away; nevertheless, his work is conceived always in the spirit of poetry." And in a rare personal reference, in "The Apparitions of Oul' Darmody" (*Hillsiders*), O'Kelly himself confessed, "the shanachie took the people of Kilbeg as he found them, the good and the bad, and sometimes he liked the bad better than the good," though the classification is too modest: O'Kelly was not merely a "shanachie"; he was on occasion an accomplished artist who had absorbed into his gift the finest qualities of the wandering hearthside storyteller and heightened them by his faculty for dramatization. Few authors have been able to absorb and reproduce more convincingly than he the sense of a primitive countryside and its people (with Galway best known).

His fundamental qualities are, I think, pastoral-dramatic in kind; they can lead to intense concentrations—as in the almost-epic, though restrained, story "The Elks," with its description of a storm by the sea. Often these qualities operate through satire, obvious or semi-submerged, as in "The Shoemaker" (with its "in-

telligent as Corkmen": and why not, with men like
Frank O'Connor, Robert Gibbings, Seán O'Faoláin,
and Daniel Corkery in evidence!) ; but the satire is
never offensive, being nourished less by wit than by a
most lambent humor: that humor "almost a charity"—
whether of statement (as in a reference to Moses' angrily
breaking the tables of the Commandments as "the most
tragic destruction of a first edition that the world has
known") or of the affectionate *illumination* of character.
For to O'Kelly the human breed was, however flawed,
curiously lovable; his handling of people has a warmth
of comprehension in its large-heartedness that whispers
of a faculty possessed in fullness only by the artist who
has chewed the same bone that Chaucer worried. And,
like most of his fellows of the Irish Renaissance, he
moves most nobly when he is handling the strands of
tragedy, as—it will be recalled—Malone, who valued
the "passively meditative charm" of his work, also
sensed.

As an artist, O'Kelly need fear no comparison, however unfortunate the fact that a tragically clipped career,
not lengthened by pitiless over-exertion, did not permit
the editing and retouching most serious writers are at
pains to indulge in. The fellow author most likely to
come to my own mind when reading him is his friend
James Stephens: a fact that seems to me complimentary
to each artist and that is meant to insinuate no indebted-
ness on the part of either to the other. There was clearly,
I think, a greater anguish of genius concentrated in
Stephens, whose mind was also the more nimble of the
two; and there is in O'Kelly (I am of course not now

speaking of him as a political journalist) no evidence of the occasional fury and desolation of Stephens. Yet somehow these men seem to companion each other easily, perhaps because the capriciousness of O'Kelly's vision may be not very far removed from that of Stephens. Then, too, neither man cursed life, though one recalls that Stephens certainly cursed its cruelty. So I am sure the association is congenial—though not exclusive, since the gently ironic Frank O'Connor might well share in it, as well as the quietly accomplished Daniel Corkery.

Bibliographies

I. ANNOTATED BIBLIOGRAPHY OF O'KELLY*

N.B.: Starred titles are those of works of which O'Kelly himself presumably read final proof. The almost hopelessly dispersed journalistic and essentially noncreative material is ignored except for the note in §D.

A. Books, Broadside, Pamphlets; Anonymous Contributions to *Aftermath* . . .

*By the | Stream of Killmeen. Dublin: Sealy, Bryers & Walker, n.d. [Aug. 1906]

N.B.: A publisher's letter of 27 February 1906 apologizes for delayed reporting on MS and offers publication with division of "any profits arising from the sale" after "cost of publication" has been defrayed. The *Southern Star,* in anticipatory approval (14 July 1906), says most of the tales had been published in Irish periodicals, with some "republished" in *it.* Oddly, O'Kelly misdates this volume 1902, in a 30 June 1915 letter to Ernest Boyd (Healy).

---

*Editor's Note: Departing from the standard selective bibliographic framework of the series, this invaluable annotated bibliography, an integral part of the monograph, is definitive and comprehensive.

Contents: "A Broken Bramble": Presumably earlier published; where, undetermined.—As 3-act play, "His Father's Son," with Acts I & III labeled as such, in *Sinn Féin,* 15 Dec. 1906, 5 & 12 Jan. 1907.

"Thade Furey's Return": Retold as "A Golden Memory," C.T.S.I. Pamphlet, No. 863.

"The Story of a Spell": As "An Evening in Cape Clear / The Story of a Spell," *The Irish Rosary,* Feb. 1905; as " 'The Next Parish to America.' / The Story of a Spell," *Donahoe's Magazine* (Boston, Mass.) , Feb. 1907. (Cf. letter from *Donahoe's,* 30 Dec. 1907: N.L. MS 2112.)

"Kate Keary's Romance."

"Was It As Well?"

"A Tragedy and a Triumph": *The Irish Rosary,* Jan. 1905.

"Fairy Gold": As "How Mickaleen Paid the Rent for Christmas" (though herein the storyteller is "Old Seaghan") , *The Irish Packet,* 17 Dec. 1904. (O'Kelly once tried to dramatize this.)

"A Land of Loneliness": As "A Land of Loneliness and How It Was Peopled," *United Irishman,* 13 Aug. 1904 (also in *Sinn Féin,* 26 Feb. 1910) .

"The Harvestman's Woman": Returned at author's request by *Irish Packet* on 16 Mar. 1906 (N.L. MS 2112) .

"The Matchmaker's Match": *Irish Weekly Independent,* 2 Dec. 1905; source of *The Matchmakers,* as earlier noticed by Mercier (Doctoral Diss., pp. 45 & 126) .— N.L. MS 1411 has incomplete combination of slightly corrected cuttings and MS.

*The Matchmakers / A Comedy in One Act. Dublin: M. H. Gill & Son, Ltd., 1908.—"New Edition" published by "The Leinster Leader, Ltd.," Naas, n.d. (Play reissued by James Duffy & Co., Dublin, 1950.) —Included in *Three Plays* (see below) .—*N.B.:* On source, see *By*

the Stream of Killmeen, above.; a Sw MS contains a large portion of the play.—First performed by Theatre of Ireland in Abbey Theatre, 13 Dec. 1907; later, in Large Concert Hall of the Rotunda (Dublin), 11 and 13 Nov. 1909.—Apparently wrongly assigned to *United Irishman* in Sw MS of what is obviously a first draft of Michael O'Kelly's "Preface" for *The Parnellite.*

*The Shuiler's Child / A Tragedy in Two / Acts. Dublin: Maunsel & Co., Ltd., 1909.

N.B.: First performance in Rotunda, 29 Apr. 1909, by Theatre of Ireland; first performance by Irish National Theatre Society, Ltd., Abbey Theatre, 24 Nov. 1910.— According to Mercier (Doctoral Diss., p. 146), translated into Irish, 1913.

*The Bard on the Bodach. Cuala Press Broadside, illustrated by Jack B. Yeats, Mar. 1912.—Cf. *Ranns & Ballads,* below.

*Three Plays. Dublin: M. H. Gill & Son, Ltd., 1912.

Contents: "The Homecoming": As "The Home-Coming. / An Incident," *Sinn Féin,* 28 Aug. 1909. (See *Waysiders,* below.)

N.B.: First performed 28 Mar. 1910 by Theatre of Ireland, Molesworth Hall, Dublin.

"The Stranger": Reworking of never-published play, "The Flame on the Hearth" (according to the *Leader,* cited below, "written partly in that language which people don't speak in Wicklow"), which had been given a lame production 24 Nov. 1908 at the Abbey Theatre by the Theatre of Ireland, with a more successful one following at the Rotunda on 19 Mar. 1909 (Cf. the *Leader,* 28 Nov. 1908; *Freeman's Journal,* 20 Mar. 1909; Nic Shiubhlaigh, 204).—*N.B.:* No record of performance of "The Stranger" has been found.

"The Matchmakers": See above.

*The Bribe / A Play in Three Acts. Dublin and London: Maunsel & Co., Ltd., 1914 [Ed. in grey boards sup-

posedly later: cf. O'Hegarty; play copy. 1914 by author].
(Play reissued by Duffy, Dublin, 1952.) *N.B.:* N.L. MS
418: Really a TS, with only 31 pp. (to end of Act I)
numbered; one p. included in Sw MSS.—First produced
18 Dec. 1913, at Abbey Theatre, by National Theatre
Society, Ltd.

*The Lady of / Deerpark. London: Methuen & Co., Ltd.,
20 Sept. 1917. *N.B.:* Mercier was the first to point out
that the "germ" of this novel was a short story, "The
House of the Heffernans," in which "Tom Kelleher" (a
recurrent O'Kelly character) has the part corresponding
to that of Jennings in the novel, published in the Christmas 1909 number of the *Irish Weekly Independent;* he
also remarked that Seumas O'Sullivan, to whom the
book was dedicated, had a proof copy: cf. Diss., 156.—
There are scattered pp. of MS and large portions of TS
among the Sw papers.

* Waysiders / Stories of Connacht. Dublin: The Talbot
Press, Ltd.; London: T. Fisher Unwin, n.d. [A publisher's letter, dated 20 Sept. 1917, in the Sw file, names
1 Oct. as the publication date]; N.Y.: Frederick A.
Stokes Co., 1919.—*N.B.:* Mercier (Diss., 166–67) says a
second ed. of this book, issued by the Talbot Press in
1924 (evidently in its "New Era Library," though undated), adds another story, "The House of the Wise
Man." I have not seen this ed., but have read the story
in reprint form in *The Hearthstone,* Oct. 1931.

Contents: "The Can with the Diamond Notch": *Sinn Féin,*
16 Apr. 1910; cf. version, "The Diamond Notch," *Irish
Weekly Independent,* 10 Dec. 1910.—Sw MSS contain a
portion.

"Both Sides of the Pond": There is a corrected Sw TS.

"The White Goat": N.L. MS 1411. (Rejected by *The
Smart Set* in 1915: Healy.)

"The Sick Call": Manchester *Guardian,* 13 Sept. 1912.

"The Shoemaker": Manchester *Guardian,* 12 Jan. 1917.

—There is an incomplete Sw MS, including the final p. of the tale, concerning Padna, a shoemaker, and the latter's story of Gobstown and its good landlord.

"The Rector": Manchester *Guardian,* 23 Apr. 1913.

"The Home-Coming": Rpt. fr. *Three Plays, q.v.*

"A Wayside Burial": Manchester *Guardian,* 22 June 1916.—N.L. MS 1411; also fragments, plus printed copy, in Sw MSS.—Story also in *Sunday Independent,* 27 Aug. 1916.—Cf. §C, 2: "The Parish Priest," below.

"The Gray Lake": There are fragmentary Sw MSS, as well as a complete Sw MS entitled "Shoemaker" [in which a shoemaker tells Padna of the drowning of a town by the "Seven Sisters" when they are released by a shepherd from their wells to permit them to meet their lover, the moon, the shepherd's reward being the daughter of the "Keeper of the Key" to the great metal cover to the wells (normally locked at night), with him and the girl, as lonely survivors, becoming progenitors of all later inhabitants of the town, including Padna himself and the shoemaker]: this has elaborate and complicated parallels and semi-parallels in fragments of Sw MS entitled "The Gray Lake."

"The Building": *Irish Weekly Independent,* 16 Nov. 1912, and *Sunday Independent,* 17 Nov. 1912.

?*The Leprechaun / of Killmeen*. Dublin: Martin Lester, Ltd., n.d.; 1920 according to O'Hegarty, though I incline toward 1918 because the National Library accession stamp reads "20 Nov. 1918," even though a penciled notation in the same copy reads "1919." (Reprinted by The Leprechaun Press, Dun Laoghaire, 1964.)

N.B.: The matter of this book was originally published serially as "Mid the New Mown Hay / Exploits of a Wonderful Leprechaun" in the *Irish Weekly Independent* under the dates parenthetically indicated below.

Contents: "The Big Man of the Fairies" (5 Dec. 1908)
"Herself and the Leprechaun" (12–19 Dec. 1908)

"The Last of Martin Moran" (26 Dec. 1908)
"The Fairy Bush" (2 Jan. 1909)
"The Poplar to the Rescue" (9 Jan. 1909)
"The Crutch and the Bull" (16 Jan. 1909)

Ranns & Ballads. Dublin: The Candle Press, Dec. 1918; 450 numbered copies, frontispiece by Jack B. Yeats from Cuala broadside *The Bard on the Bodach.*—Dedicated to author's sister Nora. (Reissued 1968 by "The Seumas O'Kelly Society," Dun Laoghaire, with an introduction by Colm Cronin heavy with pretentious claims and inaccuracies.) *N.B.:* N.L. MS 4160, inaccurately stamped "Ranns and Ballads" on its spine, contains, as here ordered, MSS of the following pieces:

"The Sorrow of Drumree / (To the Memory of Francis Ledwidge)": Not in *Ranns & Ballads,* but published in *Sunday Independent,* 16 Feb. 1919. There is a Sw MS.

"The Show Man"

"The Shearers"

{ "A Claddagh Man's Story" (Title used in *Ranns & Ballads*)

("The Blessing of the Bay / A Claddagh Man's Simple Story"

"The Thatcher"

"A Fideóg Player"

"The Fair Maid" (Of a *sid* who teased a turf-cutter as a maiden, only to escape as a butterfly)

Contents (There is a one-page canceled plan among the Sw MSS) as in *R & B:*

"The Showman"

"The Shearers": *Sinn Féin,* 14 Mar. 1908.—The author has, as a gift from Mr. Sweeney, a close MS version, in two parts; there are also Sw MS variants for Stanzas 4, 6, and 7.

"The Tinker": There are Sw MSS of the last stanza, of experimental—or tentative—versions of the first stanza, and of close approximation of the first three stanzas.

"The Cabin Hunter": *Sinn Féin,* 17 Feb. 1912.—There are two canceled opening stanzas on the back of p. 106 of N.L. MS 1412; and there are Sw MSS giving tentative versions of Stanzas 1–6 and one complete draft close to the final one.

"The Fisherman": *United Irishman,* 14 Apr. 1906.— There are two Sw MSS of the first two stanzas and a variant of the last two.

"The Bard on the Bodach": Noted above, as broadside.— A Sw TS has almost exactly the same version.

"A Fideóg Player": *Nationality,* 17 Feb. 1917.

"The Ballad of the Twelve Marys": *Irish Review,* July 1912.—There are 12 stanzas in corrected Sw TSS.

"The Thatcher": *Sinn Féin,* 13 Feb. 1909.—There is a Sw TS.

"The Lazy Wall" [Salthill, Galway, according to a Sw MS, the evidence of which suggests "By a Seaside Wall" as an earlier title]:

"I. The Widower": Various Sw MSS: one has the final title; another has an earlier, "The Widower on the Look Out Again"; a third has further variants; a fourth is a tentative version written on the back of a sheet from *The Weaver's Grave* MS.

"II. An Sean-Fhear"

"III. The Revolutionary"

"IV. Patsy Na Mallacht": One Sw MS, "Patsy the Growler," offers an early form of the first stanza, while a second approximates the final version.

"V. The Maid of All Work": Sw MS has early version entitled "IX The Servant Girl at a Lodging-house Window."

"VI. The Tram Horse": There is a Sw MS.

"VII. A Pinch of Snuff"

"VIII. The Cockle Sellers"

"IX. The Shanachie Tells Another Story": From

Aftermath of Easter Week, q.v.—A Sw MS entitled "What the Shanachie Saw" has obviously the earliest version.

"The Stone Breakers": A Sw MS has the first three stanzas in variant form.

"The Spinner": There is a Sw TS of the first four stanzas, corresponding closely to final form.

"A Claddagh Man's Story": Cf. *"N.B.",* above.—A Sw MS has the first three stanzas.

"Castle O'Neill": Sw MSS have two discarded early versions, one fairly close to final form.

"Mad Sarah": A Sw MS entitled "Mad Sally" has some variant forms.

"The Little Branch": *Sinn Féin,* 26 Dec. 1908.—One Sw MS has only the conclusion; another has a full version with minor variations.

"A Mourner of the Famine Days": Eight stanzas of an earlier draft entitled "The Mourner" exist among the Sw MSS, also two in a Sw TS; a version entitled "The Mourner" may be found in *Sinn Féin,* 7 Jan. 1911.

"A Cradle Song": There is a Sw MS of the original version in four stanzas; cf. "Husho," *United Irishman,* 18 Nov. 1905.

"Slan Leat": The author has a MS version presented by Mr. Sweeney.

Meadowsweet. / A Comedy, in One Act. Naas: "The Leinster Leader, Ltd.," n.d. [1919]; also Dublin: The Talbot Press, Ltd., n.d. *N.B.:* First produced 7 Oct. 1919, at Abbey Theatre, by Irish National Theatre Society, Ltd.; one or two fragments preserved in Sw MSS.—Source clearly in a short story, "On the Rise of the Hill" (Sw MS), "Jim Rafferty" changed to "Johnny Claffey" and "Katie Hogan" to "Maria Dempsey," and a conflict between two landowners incorporated, with Johnny emerging as Maria's master in the end.

The Parnellite | A Play in Three Acts. Naas: "The Lein-
ster Leader, Ltd.," n.d. [1919]

    N.B.: First produced 24 Sept. 1917, at Abbey Theatre, by
Irish National Theatre Society, Ltd.—N.L. MS 1410,
entitled "Kilmacshane," with separate pagination of
each of the three acts, appears to be the original of
what became *The Parnellite.* Another N.L. "MS,"
No. 417, really a 132-page TS, is entitled "The Parnellite" and has the original title, "Kilmacshane," crossed
out, but a letter from J. A. Keogh, of the Abbey (N.L.
MS 2112), shows the play was submitted for production under the title "Kilmacshane." There is a fragmentary Sw MS perhaps representing the earliest
draft, possibly to be associated with several other Sw
MSS (*e.g.,* on reverse sides of "Shoemaker" sheets and
of what is a portion of the story "Nan") that chal-
lenge, perhaps hopelessly, ordering and clarification.
(One of the few fruitful sources of biographical information is the preface to the published play, by
O'Kelly's brother Michael, dated "Naas, June, 1919.")

The | Golden Barque | and | The | Weaver's Grave.
Dublin: The Talbot Press Ltd., and London: T. Fisher
Unwin Ltd., 1919; N.Y.: G. P. Putnam's Sons, 1920.—
Separate edition of *The Weaver's Grave,* with eight
illustrations by Jack B. Yeats, published by Talbot
Press and Unwin, n.d. [1922: date of N.L. acquisition
stamp]—Strangely, *The Golden Barque* is listed as already published on the title-page of *Waysiders,* suggesting composition prior to Sept. 1917.

"The Golden Barque": Though later revised and reor-
dered, to my own knowledge serially published as parenthetically numbered below in the *Sunday Independent,*
23 June–28 July 1912, though the director of the National Library informs me (16 Aug. 1967) that it also
appeared in the *Irish Weekly Independent* for 22 and 29
June and 5, 13, and 27 July.

(1) "Michael and Mary": 23 June issue.—Mr. Sweeney has cuttings of corrected copy in newsprint, preceded by one MS page of text and another containing the general title, "The Golden Barque."

(2) "Hike and Calcutta": 30 June.—Entitled "Hike" in newspaper version.—N.L. MS 1411 consists mainly of much-revised newspaper cuttings.

(3) "The Haven": 7 July, but earlier (24 April 1912) in Manchester *Guardian*.—N.L. MS 1411 has a combination of revised newspaper cuttings and MS.

(5) "Billy the Clown": 21 July.—Entitled "Mickey" in newspaper version; "Micky and the Terror" in N.L. MS 1411, which is, again, a mixture of MS and corrected printed copy.

(6) "The Derelict": 28 July.—Entitled "The Affair of James Vesey" ["Vasey" in text] in newspaper version; "The Derelict and His Daughter" in N.L. MS 1411, which contains a large portion of pasted-in printed copy. One page of TS is among the Sw materials.

(4) "The Man with the Gift": 14 July.

"The Weaver's Grave": N.L. MS 1412: incomplete, autographed MS, "The Weaver's Grave: A Story of Old Men": 108 numbered pages, breaking off with " 'The nearest elm tree I know,' said"; several interpolated sheets with bits of verse (*e.g.*, a canceled p. 8 has on its reverse side several stanzas beginning "The mother waiting . . .") . Mr. Sweeney has other MS-portions.

N.B.: In the reception lobby of Radio Éireann (Henry St., Dublin 1) hangs (1967) a plaque (with reproduction in colored enamel on bronze of a Jack B. Yeats illustration: see above) commemorating the award of the *Prix Italia*, 1961, to the station for a radio adaptation of *The Weaver's Grave* made by Micheál ó hAodha (Productions Director, Radio Telefís Éireann) and performed by R. É players. The TS of the adaptation, generously loaned for examination by

Mr. ó hAodha, runs to 44 pp. exclusive of the "Explanatory Note."

Hillsiders. Dublin: The Talbot Press, Ltd.; London: T. Fisher Unwin, Ltd., 1921.

> *N.B.:* Originally issued, with stories running in the order parenthetically indicated below, as "Hearts among the Hills" (the title from a phrase in "The Elks"), in the *Irish Weekly Independent,* 13 Mar.– 5 June 1909.—The proposed title "Hillsiders & Others" is recorded, though without indication of proposed book-content, in N.L. MS 1411, on the reverse of p. 79 of "Micky and the Terror" (*i.e.,* "Billy the Clown" in *The Golden Barque* . . .).

Contents: (4) "Hannah": in *I. W. I.,* "IV–Hannah," 8 May 1909.

> (1) "The Prodigal Daughter": The series begins in *I. W. I.* under its general title, 13 Mar. 1909, with Ch. I and part of Ch. II; the latter is continued 20 Mar. under the title "I.–The Prodigal Daughter"; and the story is concluded 27 Mar. as "I.–The Prodigal Daughter / III."
>
> (2) "The Miracle of the Tea": In *I. W. I.,* "II.–The Miracle of the Tea," begun 3 Apr. with Ch. I and part of Ch. II, and concluded 10 Apr. with continuation of Ch. II + Ch. III.
>
> (5) "Nan Hogan's House": In *I. W. I.,* "V.–Nan Hogan's House," Ch. I, 15 May; "Second Installment / Chapter Two," 22 May; "Third . . . / . . . III," 29 May.—There is a one-page Sw MS.
>
> (3) "The Elks": In *I. W. I.:* Ch. I, 17 Apr., as "III.– The Elks"; Ch. II, 24 Apr.; Ch. III, 1 May.
>
> (6) "The Apparitions of Oul' Darmody": in *I. W. I.,* "VI.–The Apparitions . . . ," 5 June.

Wet Clay. Dublin: The Talbot Press, Ltd. & London: T. Fisher Unwin, Ltd., 1922; N.Y. (though printed in Ireland) : Frederick A. Stokes Co., 1923.—Also in "Library of Modern Irish Fiction," Dublin: Phoenix Pub. Co., n.d.

N.B.: Serially published, *Irish Weekly Independent,* 12 Mar.–22 Oct. 1921.—N.L. MS 416: 3 vols. + box: has name and address (6, Home Farm Road, Drumcondra, Dublin) on title-page. The first ten chapters occupy 304 lined sheets; they are followed by two chapters written on larger lined sheets and ending on p. 356 with "Then who has he married—or who has ventured to marry him?" The rest of the MS is on sheets, lined and unlined, of varying size. Chs. 13–19 are separately bound; Chs. 14 and 15 consist of galleys, as does part of Ch. 17 also. Chs. 20–27 are also separately bound and end with "Brendan Nilan lay at full length on his back on the brown earth." The box, labeled "416 Part IV," contains many miscellaneous sheets of MS, thrown together in no apparent order.— The Sw file has many MS sheets, as well as one page ("35") on the reverse side of a sheet containing a partial draft of "The Cabin Hunter" (*Ranns & Ballads*) .

PAMPHLETS:

A Golden Memory: Dublin: Catholic Truth Society of Ireland Pamphlet No. 863, n.d.—"Thade Furey's Return" (*By the Stream of Killmeen*) , retitled.

The Revenge of Seaghan Buidhe: Id., Pamphlet No. 936, 1928.—Serially pub. in the *Weekly Freeman,* 17–24 Mar. 1923.—N.L. MS 9898: 65 pp.

The Marriage Money & An Island Eve: Id., Pamphlet No. 938, 1928. "The Marriage Money": In *Irish Weekly Independent,* Christmas no., 1907.—Sw file has this in MS combined with corrected news type. "An Island Eve": In *Irish Weekly Independent,* Christmas no., 1918.

ANONYMOUS CONTRIBUTIONS to *Aftermath of Easter Week* (Dublin: Published for the Irish National Aid and

Volunteers' Dependents Fund, Sept. 1917; "Foreword" by P[atrick] B[rowne]: cf. *Adventures of an Irish Bookman,* ed. Francis Mac Manus, Dublin: Talbot Press, 1952; pp. 187–88) .—To this quickly-British-suppressed booklet of 15 anonymous lyrics (really by Father Browne, Seumas O'Sullivan, Oliver St. John Gogarty, *et al.*) , O'Kelly contributed three:

"The Seanachie Tells Another Story": Later in *Ranns & Ballads;*

"The Boreen, 1916": There is a Sw TS;

"Piper Denis Delany": There is a Sw MS.

B. Collaboration

"Lustre": Regarded as a collaboration—confirmed in a 12 January 1915 letter from O'Kelly to Ernest Boyd (Healy)—between O'Kelly and Count Casimir de Markievicz, husband of Constance (neé Gore-Booth) and author of the later "The Memory of the Dead" (concerned with the 1798 rising and produced by the "Independent Dramatic Co.," Dublin) , the style suggests O'Kelly pure and simple. Amateur production of "Lustre" seems indicated by a 23 Feb. 1930 letter to O'Kelly's sister Nora, preserved in N.L. MS 2112 (which also has a 5 Mar. 1908 letter from Seumas Connolly which refers to the coming "Monday night" production of "Markievicz's play") . Typed notes shown the writer by Mr. Sweeney, and attributed to Count Markievicz' son, have "About the same time—1908–9 he [O'Kelly] and my father, wrote 'LUSTRE' or 'The Lustre Jug' . . . my father's first dramatic effort. . . . It is the least known of the works of both its collaborators . . . ," with a succeeding "Chronology of Literary productions" which dates "Lustre" 1907, though a correction in pen suggests "late" 1907 "or 1908."

Among the many fragmentary Sw MSS is one comprising a large segment of "Lustre"; the play, with authorship attributed to O'Kelly alone, was printed in the Christmas 1920 number of the *Irish Weekly Independent* in a version which differs in some minor respects from the complete TS presented to the writer by Mr. Sweeney, and edited for publication in *Éire- Ireland,* II, 4 (Winter 1967–68), unfortunately before the editor had learned of O'Kelly's having dated his collaboration 1913 in a 30 June 1915 letter to Ernest Boyd (Healy). The play, according to another letter to Boyd (26 August 1915: Healy), was rejected by *The Smart Set.*

C, 1. Lost, Uncollected, or Partly Preserved Creative Matter of Possible Interest, including MSS and TSS

1. *Matter Demonstrably Published, in Whole or in Part*

"On Galway Bay" (Verse) : *United Irishman,* 8 July 1905.

"An Autumn Impression" (Verse) : *Irish Rosary,* Nov. 1905.

"Husho" (Verse) : *United Irishman,* 18 Nov. 1905.

"An Ologone" (Verse lament for death of a girl) : *United Irishman,* 20 Jan. 1906.

"A Quest" (Verse) : *Sinn Féin,* 26 Sept. 1908.

"The House of the Heffernans": See *The Lady of Deerpark,* above.

"At the Burning of the Sod / Further Adventures of a Wonderful Leprechaun": *Irish Weekly Independent,* 12 Mar.–16 Apr. 1910:

12 Mar. story untitled
19 Mar.: "II—The Capture"
26 Mar.: "III—The Caves"
2 Apr.: "IV—The Big Hunt"
9 Apr.: "V—The Shipwreck"
16 Apr.: "VI—The Good Red Gold"

N.B.: Sequel to *The Leprechaun of Killmeen, q.v.*

"The Triumph of Living" (Story) : *Summer Magazine,* 1911 (Credible assignment: periodical not available to writer) : Sw TS.—Cf. editorial request from T. F. O'Sullivan, N.L. MS 2112.

"Wild Blood" (Ballad) : Christmas 1911 no. (dated 2 Dec.) , *Irish Weekly Independent,* p. 10.

Further "Padna" Tales:

"A Day by the Lake": Manchester *Guardian,* 22 Aug. 1916 (Rpt., *Irish Weekly Independent,* 4 Oct. 1919, & *Sunday Independent,* 5 Oct. 1919) .

"Padna and the Rope": Manchester *Guardian,* 2 Oct. 1916 (Rpt., entitled "Padna and the Old Soldier," Christmas 1917 no., *Irish Weekly Independent*) .— There is a one-page Sw MS headed "Padna and His Rope."

"The House of Nan": Manchester *Guardian,* 19 Oct. 1916 (Rpt., entitled "Nan," *Irish Weekly Independent,* 30 Aug. 1919, & *Sunday Independent,* 31 Aug. 1919) .—There is a fragmentary Sw MS of 7 pp. concerning Padna in the "house of Nan."

"The Sun Lover": *Irish Weekly Independent,* 2 Dec. 1916.—There is a Sw TS.

"Mushrooms": Manchester *Guardian,* 24 Aug. 1917 (Rpt., *Sunday Independent,* 27 July 1919) .

"The Golden Wren": *Weekly Freeman,* 8 Dec. 1917.— Galley proof in Sw file.

"Padna Mitches": *Sunday Independent,* 30 Nov. 1919.

"Padna at the Play": *Irish Weekly Independent,* 31 Jan. 1920; *Sunday Independent,* 1 Feb. 1920.

"The Sorrow of Drumree" and "The Fair Maid": See *Ranns & Ballads,* above.

"The Old Gray Lake" (Verse) : *Shamrock,* 8 Mar. 1919. —There is a Sw TS. Cf. Sw MS "Lough Rea."

"The Celtic Temperament" (Story) : *Irish Weekly Independent,* 8–15–22 May 1920.—There are Sw MSS of both a large portion of the story and of its recasting as a one-act play: basically a wooden effort to proselytize in favor of the Irish language.

"To One in America" (Verse) : *Irish Weekly Independent,* Christmas 1921 no.—There is a Sw TS, as well as a corrected TS entitled "A Verse Epistle to One in America."

"Edain / A Romance of the Days of the Druids": First six chapters only published in *Weekly Freeman,* 30 Dec. 1922; some 80 pp. (including the final two) of the 273 pp. of this MS are among the Sw MSS, the 80 pp. beginning with Ch. VII of the story.

"Driftwood" (1-Act Play) : To date (1967) not issued in book form, but published in the *Dublin Magazine,* I, 4 (Sept. 1923) . 287–306.

> *N.B.:* N.L. MS 415: 73 pp. in strict MS form; title-page carries the address on the MS of *Wet Clay.*—First produced by Miss A. E. F. Horniman's repertory company on 11 Oct. 1915 at the Gaiety Theatre, Manchester, England; later (10 Jan. 1916) at the Duke of York's Theatre, London. (N.L. MS 2112 has a touching 14 July 1915 letter from Miss Horniman to O'Kelly, as well as his cordial and amusing 20 July reply.)

"A Dream Sea" (Verse) : *Irish Independent,* 19 June 1924.—There is a Sw MS.

"The Optimist" (Verse) : *Irish Weekly Independent,* 15 Mar. 1924.—There is a Sw TS.

"In Bodenstown" (Verse) : *The Distributive Worker,* Apr. 1926 (Assignment: periodical not available to the writer) .

> *N.B.:* Cf. also "Anonymous Contributions to *Aftermath . . . ,*" §A, and "Collaboration," §B, above.

C, 2. Other Matter

"On the Rise of the Hill" (Short Story) : Sw MS.—Conceivably published; if so, place and date undetermined.

"The Parish Priest": 10-page N.L. MS 1411: Less a

story than a record of attendance at the burial of "Martin Doolan," who died a ruined and drunken pauper after breaking under the "land war."—Cf. "A Wayside Burial," *Waysiders,* above.

"Lough Rea" (Verse) : Sw MS.

"Spring and the Rose": Sw MS of some pages of this 3-act comedy a bit pontifically rejected by Yeats for Abbey production in a letter of 29 Feb. 1912 (also in Sw file) .

"Going to the Christmas Market," signed "Seumas O Ceallaig": Sw TS of a brief, sentimental "tear-jerker."

"To Elis" (Love Lyric) : Sw MS.

"The Tragedy" (Lyric) : Sw MS.—Cf. verses on back of pp. 103 & 104, N.L. MS 1412.

"To One in Connacht" (Verse) : Sw MS.

"The Moonlighters / The Boy; / The Girl": Sw MS of two trivial bits of verse.

Untitled Verse ("Or looking out with pilgrim gaze") : Sw MS: Obviously conclusion of longer piece.

Untitled page of verse in Sw TS reminiscent of a boyhood friendship.

"By a Seaside Wall: I The Dreamer" (Verse) : Mildly satiric Sw MS.

"The Poorhouse Gate (The Prayer of an Old Woman of the Roads) " (Verse) : Sw MS.

"In Memory (Autumn, 1906) ": Sw MS of imperfect, though sincere, verse anent "her" who "sleeps beside the lake."

"To a Singer": Sw MS of a lyric to a bird (somewhat above O'Kelly's average) .

"Ye Olde Salt" (Verse) : Sw MS.

"The Ballad of Sheela Gaul": Sw file contains 2 pp. of MS and 1 of TS apparently belonging to this ballad; they are seemingly related to verses on the back of a canceled p. 8 in N.L. MS 1412 (of the incomplete *Weaver's Grave*) , and they may suggest a serious loss, since, though imperfect, they are not unexciting, O'Kelly having been far from his worst in the ballad form.

D. Note on Fugitive Prose, with Selected Titles

How much material in the form of unsigned editorials, reportorial journalism whether or not signed, personal essays of a sort, etc. may be concealed in the various journals edited, or contributed to, by O'Kelly is anybody's guess. The many identified or clearly assignable pieces seen by the writer do not—despite the incidental charm of some essays (especially those showing concern with birds), the satiric piquancy of certain political or social commentaries, etc.—suggest a significant creative loss in permitting their matter to remain (as inevitably much of it must) in its literary limbo: basically, all but a few are just superior journalism.

The pieces listed below, most of them chosen from some eighty contributed to the *Sunday Independent* (1917–19), would seem fairly suggestive of scope and quality in this miscellaneous category:

"The Greatest Fair in the Kingdom" [Ballinasloe]: *Irish Packet,* 15 Oct. 1904.

"The Greatest of the Schools of Ancient Erin" [Clonmacnoise]: *Irish Rosary,* Dec. 1905.

"A Skirmish": Manchester *Guardian,* 3 July 1912.

"In a City Square": Manchester *Guardian,* 27 Nov. 1912 (Also in *Sunday Independent* for both 1 Sept. 1917 and 6 July 1919).

"The Emigrant Train": Manchester *Guardian,* 12 Jan. 1916.

"The Blight": Manchester *Guardian,* 30 Mar. 1917.

"Dublin in Modern Literature": *Sunday Independent,* 30 Sept. 1917.

"The Seagull": Manchester *Guardian,* 10 Oct. 1917 (Also *Sunday Independent,* 28 Oct. 1917).

"The Mouse": Manchester *Guardian,* 18 Mar. 1918.

"Coming of the Corncrake": *Sunday Independent,* 12 May 1918.

"An Autumn Morning": *Sunday Independent,* 22 Sept. 1918.

"The Swan Song": *Nationality,* 16 Nov. 1918: N.L. MS 4159–60.

"Spring in the Garden" ["By Gallimh (the Late Seumas O' Kelly) "]: *Sunday Independent,* 13 Apr. 1919.

"La Grippe": *Sunday Independent,* 11 May 1919.

"A Tinker's Skirmish": *Sunday Independent,* 15 June 1919.

"The Apple Woman": *Sunday Independent,* 7 Sept. 1919.

"Bird-Catching—and Its Cruelty": *Sunday Independent,* 5 Oct. 1919.

II. SELECTIVE BIBLIOGRAPHY OF SECONDARY WORKS

Anon. "In Loughrea and South Galway." *Connacht Tribune,* 17 Aug. 1935.

―――― "Seumas O'Kelly." *Literary Supplement to "The Gael,"* 28 Aug. 1922.

―――― "Death of Mr. Seumas O'Kelly." *Leinster Leader,* 16 Nov. 1918. (Presumably by Michael O'Kelly.)

Boyd, E. A. *Ireland's Literary Renaissance,* rev. ed. N.Y.: Knopf, 1922.

―――― *The Contemporary Drama of Ireland.* Dublin: Talbot Press; London: Unwin, 1918.

Brennan, R. *Allegiance.* Dublin: Browne and Nolan, 1950.

Figgis, Darrell. "Seumas O'Kelly." *Shamrock,* 20 Nov. 1920.

Grennan, E. "The Short Stories of Seumas O'Kelly." Master's Thesis, University College, Dublin (1964).

Gwynn, S. "Modern Irish Literature." *Manchester Guardian Commercial,* 15 Mar. 1923.

Healy: Four Letters from O'Kelly to Ernest Boyd, now in the collection of James A. Healy.

Mc Guire, J. B. "Realism in Irish Drama." Doctoral Diss., Trinity College, Dublin.

Malone, A. E. "The Decline of the Irish Drama." *Dublin Magazine,* May 1924.

———— *The Irish Drama.* London: Constable, 1929.

———— "Seumas O'Kelly." *Dublin Magazine,* July-Sept. 1930.

Mercier, V. "Realism in Anglo-Irish Fiction 1916–1940." Doctoral Diss., Trinity College, Dublin.

Morton, David. "Literature and Life / A Neglected Talent." *Irish Statesman,* 3 Aug. 1929.

na h-Eireann, Lile. "The Humour of Seumas O'Kelly." *Greann,* Feb. 1925.

N.L. MSS: National Library of Ireland MSS [*N.B.:* The O'Kelly MSS in the N.L. (1967) are numbered as follows: 415, 416, 417, 418, 1410, 1411, 1412, 2112, 3208, 4159–60, 9898].

Nic Shiubhlaigh, Máire. *The Splendid Years / Recollections . . . as Told to Edward Kenny.* Dublin: Duffy, 1955.

O'Hanlon, A. "Literary Musings." *Irish Independent,* 1 Mar. 1947.

———— "Seumas O'Kelly / 1880–1918." *The Capuchin Annual,* 1949.

O'Hegarty, P. S. *A Bibliography of Books by Seumas O'Kelly.* "Printed for the author by" Alex. Thom & Co., Ltd., 1934 [25 copies: fr. *Dublin Magazine*].

O'Kelly, M. "Homage to Seumas O'Kelly" (25th anniversary of death) : Radio Éireann Broadcast, 16 Nov. 1943.

———— Preface to *The Parnellite* (Naas: "The Leinster Leader, Ltd.," n.d. [1919]) .

O'Sullivan, Seumas [*James Starkey*]. *Essays and Recollections.* Dublin and Cork: Talbot Press, 1944. (Cf. "Seumas O'Kelly," *Irish Times,* 13 Nov. 1943.)

———— "Seumas O'Kelly. His Work and His Personality." *Sunday Independent* (Dublin) , 17 Nov. 1918.

———— "The Late Mr. Seumas O'Kelly." *Leinster Leader,* 23 Nov. 1918. (Cf. *Irish Independent,* 18 Nov. 1918.)

———— *The Rose and Bottle and Other Essays.* Dublin: Talbot Press, 1946.

Reid, Forrest. *Retrospective Adventures.* London: Faber and Faber, 1942.

———— Review of *Golden Barque* ... *Irish Statesman,* 6 Dec. 1919.

Rose, M. G. "An Irish Widow of Ephesus ..." *Éire-Ireland,* Spring 1967.

Saul, George Brandon. "The Short Stories of Seumas O'Kelly." N.Y. Public Library *Bulletin,* Apr. 1963.—Rev. for *Rushlight Heritage.* Philadelphia: Walton Press, 1969.

———— "The Verse, Novels, and Drama of Seumas O'Kelly." *Éire-Ireland,* Spring 1967.

Sw: MSS, TSS, Letters, etc. in possession (1967) of O'Kelly's nephew, Mr. Alphonsus Sweeney, of Dun Laoghaire, Co. Dublin, Ireland.

Victory, L. H. "Seumas O'Kelly, Poet." *Sunday Independent,* 19 Oct. 1919.